COMPACT
CYMRU

C000109181

Creating

An artist's exploration of the capital

Mary Traynor

Gwasg Carreg Gwalch

First published in 2020
© text and her own illustrations: Mary Traynor

ISBN: 978-1-84524-296-1

Cover design: Eleri Owen

Published by Gwasg Carreg Gwalch,
12 Iard yr Orsaf, Llanrwst, Wales LL26 0EH
tel: 01492 642031
email: books@carreg-gwalch.cymru
website: www.carreg-gwalch.cymru

previous page: Cardiff University from Museum Avenue.

Some animals from Cardiff Castle wall.

Contents

The Stadium in 1999 ready to take Cardiff into the space age.

Introduction

My English perception of Cardiff was naive until I married a Welshman and came to live here. I had thought Cardiff was a city way over in a distant corner of Britain, surrounded by coal mines and famous for winning international rugby matches at Cardiff Arms Park. The Welsh had their own language, were great singers, especially of hymns, ate leeks and wore the daffodil on St David's Day. It rained a lot, as indeed it still does.

When I moved to Cardiff in 1962, I immediately saw that it was a fascinating historical city. Yes, there were coal mines, but they were northwards in the Valleys and without them Cardiff would not have grown from a small market town into a large metropolis during the 19th and early 20th centuries. I was, and still am, excited by it all and have focussed my artistic practice on Cardiff.

By 1962 however, two world wars and a declining coal industry were taking their toll. Cardiff Docks, once the largest coal exporter in the world, were only a shadow of their former selves. Areas of the city were being redeveloped and new road systems introduced. Besides my ongoing work, I began to feverishly record with sketchbooks and camera the buildings threatened by demolition and redevelopment, a record now held at the Glamorgan Archives in Cardiff. I also joined The Victorian Society and Cardiff Civic Society to help in the conservation of Cardiff's best historic buildings.

This book is not a straightforward history of Cardiff. I could not write that, and it has been done by fine historians whose writing is gratefully acknowledged. It is a personal account of Cardiff, choosing aspects of particular interest to me, the way one artist and architectural sleuth sees the city. As I explored Cardiff I grew familiar with the group of busy Victorian and Edwardian architects: E.M.W. Corbett the Bute Estate architect of many buildings on Bute owned land; John Prichard who carried out the 19th century restoration of Llandaff Cathedral; Edwin Rickards of the City Hall and Law Courts; Col. Bruce Vaughan; Edwin Seward of the Coal Exchange and of course the '*strange genius*'[1] William Burges who created the Gothic fantasies of Cardiff Castle and Castell Coch.

Key to Map

1. Cardiff Castle
2. Animal Wall & Pettigrew's
3. Blackfriars Priory site
4. Royal Welsh College of Music & Drama and Burges Stables
5. Cardiff University Buildings
6. Alexandra Gardens with Wales War Memorial and other memorials
7. Cardiff Law Courts
8. Cardiff City Hall
9. National Museum of Wales
10. No. 20 Park Place – Park House
11. Church of Dewi Sant
12. City United Reformed Church
13. New Theatre and former Institute of Engineers
14. The Chapel Restaurant
15. St David's Cathedral
16. Midland Bank
17. Queen's Chambers
18. Castle, High Street and Duke Street Arcades
19. Church of St John the Baptist
20. Old Library
21. Morgan Arcade
22. Royal Arcade
23. Wyndham Arcade
24. Golden Cross Pub
25. Jacob's Market
26. Prince of Wales or Wetherspoon's
27. Principality Stadium
28. W.R.U. Store
29. Queen's Vault Pub
30. Angel Hotel
31. Cardiff University Department of Engineering
32. St Peter's Church
33. The Mansion House

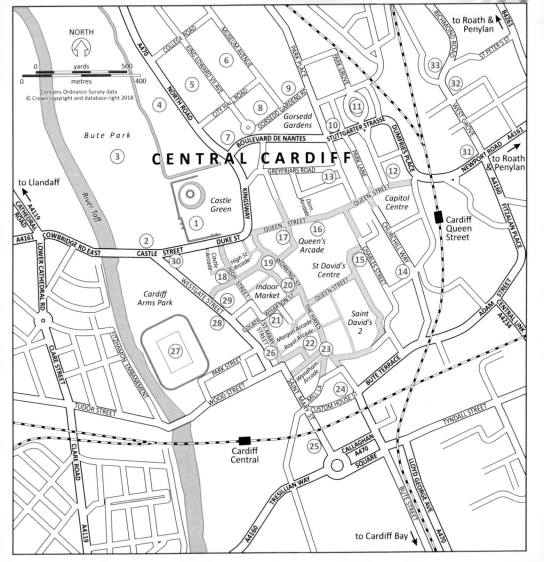

Creating Cardiff

Cardiff became a city in 1905 and the capital of Wales in 1955. It has a castle, civic buildings and extensive parklands, docks, two cathedrals, three universities, concert halls and theatres and museums. A new rugby stadium and arts centre marked the millenium. It is hard to believe that, only about a hundred and sixty years ago, this vibrant city was not much bigger than a medium sized market town. This astonishing transformation was begun with the rise of the iron and coal industries of the Glamorganshire Valleys and the wealth and enterprise of the 2nd and 3rd Marquesses of Bute who built four large docks between 1839 and 1907. The town of Cardiff grew with them resulting in an overwhelming variety of Victorian and Edwardian buildings from small terraced dwellings to larger middle class houses. Ornament abounds in stone, brick and iron: rows of chimneys, the tiles and ironwork of porches and the variety of doors and windows are a never ending source of subjects for drawings and paintings. Parks and trees enhance the townscape and capture the light and colour

Cardiff Castle: a Christmas card using one of the Burges angels from the Banqueting Hall.

of passing seasons. And of course there is the crowning glory of the Civic Centre, the Castle, Llandaff Cathedral and Cardiff Bay.

If you can, visit Cardiff University in spring when the blossom trees in Alexandra Gardens, Museum Avenue frame the front façade (see page 1). This is so long and low that I decided to do just the central part of this huge building; it is low to be like the rest of the early buildings in Cathays Park whose height was stipulated by the 3rd Marquess of Bute when he sold the land to the Town Council in 1898.

Custom House Waterguard being moved.

I could not believe my eyes when, in 1993, on one of my frequent sketching trips to Cardiff Bay I saw the Waterguard being jacked up on bricks. What a lucky moment as I could immediately record it with my note book and camera! It dates from the 1850s, and certainly looks strong enough with solid walls and battlements to deter sailors and travelers from smuggling.

The name originates from 1809 when the 'Preventive Waterguard' arm of HM Customs and Excise was set up to combat smuggling from Waterguard Watch Houses around the coast. In 1909 it was absorbed into HM Customs and Excise, which had been its Cardiff Docks office since1871. The historic building fits very well on the contemporary Waterguard pub, adding to the regeneration of Cardiff Docks.

I. The Early Centuries

Celts and Romans

Prehistoric man lived on the Glamorgan and Gwent levels but the first known people were the Celts, named the Silures by the Romans. They were, according to Roman accounts, short, stocky, with black curly hair and were very fierce defenders of their lands. They lived mainly in hilltop strongholds, but there is also evidence of their settlements around Cardiff. The story of Cardiff itself begins with the Romans. The Cardiff area was then on a large estuary where the rivers Taff and Ely entered the sea and some Celtic dwellings have been re-created at St Fagans National Museum of History near Cardiff to show how they lived. The Romans built a fort beside the river Taff and remains of the walls, dating from c.55 AD, can be seen in the present walls of Cardiff Castle outlined in pink Radyr stone, and in the café.

The Romans had left Wales by the early 5th century AD and Cardiff Castle mouldered away during the Dark Ages, the small settlement subject to attacks from marauding Irish and Vikings. It seems that some Vikings settled in Cardiff, as suggested by the names of Womanby Street, Dumballs Road and Working Street.

The Celtic Irbic Cross in Llandough Churchyard. The inscription IRBICL or 'The Stone of Irbic' appears on the base.

A reconstruction of the Roman Gate at Cardiff Castle by the 4th Marquess of Bute in 1908-21.

2. William the Conqueror to Henry VII

Cardiff Castle and its Lords, churches, the Plague, Owain Glyndŵr

After William the Conqueror defeated and killed Harold II of England in 1066, it seems that he passed through Cardiff in 1081 on his way to St David's and as he returned decided to have a motte (*mound topped with a wooden fort*) raised within a bailey (*a courtyard*) using the ruins of the Roman fort. This was the pattern of Norman attacks on Wales – infiltrate the country along lowland routes, seizing land and building mottes for their occupying forces. The Welsh would then rally and reclaim their lands and independence. This pattern of invasion and resistance lasted over 200 years. The Cardiff motte was held by Robert Fitzhammon, one of William's kinsmen, who also seized lands in Glamorgan from its king Iestyn ap Gwyrgant.

Fitzhammon died in 1107 and his daughter Mabel married Robert, a natural son of Henry I. The king granted Robert the Earldom of Gloucester and made him Lord of Glamorgan. Known as Robert the Consul, he is said to have built the present twelve-sided stone keep in the mid 12th century. He also made a grant of churches to the Benedictine monks of Tewkesbury Abbey which he founded and where he is buried. The Benedictines founded the Parish Church of St Mary the Virgin on the site of Central Station and, in 1180, the small Church of St John the Baptist became its chapel-of-ease (*a resting place for the dead before burial*). Because of increasing numbers of people living near the castle, St John's was also made a parish church in 1243 although St Mary's strongly objected, even complaining to the Pope. The Dominican Black Friars arrived in 1242 and established themselves on what is now Cooper's Field in Bute Park where the excavated remains of the Friary can be seen. The Franciscans founded a friary in 1280 at Greyfriars, now the site of the Capital Tower.

> *Cardiff castle's twelve-sided shell Keep, mid 12th century, was an advanced design for its time. The steps and its fragmentary walls are all that remain of the huge forebuilding and wall that extended from the Keep down to the Black Tower.*

The west side of Cardiff Castle showing the Gate – a reconstruction built by the 4th Marquess of Bute in between 1889 and 1923.

In 1158 William FitzRobert the Norman, who was living with a hundred of his warriors in the motte of Cardiff Castle, sent them to the court of Morgan ap Owain, Lord of Caerleon and Gwynllwg. Morgan was killed and his lands and property seized by FitzRobert's men. Shortly after that, William FitzRobert sent a strong army to Senghenydd on a similar mission. Ifor ap Meurig – known as 'Ifor Bach' ('*little Ifor*') because of his size – was the Lord of Senghenydd and although the Normans captured a large part of his estate, he and his men eluded them.

In Cardiff Castle FitzRobert felt safe and strong. But one night, Ifor Bach stealthily placed long ladders against the castle walls and he was the first over the battlements. They searched the tower in darkness and found William FitzRobert's bedroom. They tied up FitzRobert and his wife and carried them off, along with their baby son, to the mountain forests. Ifor refused to release them until the stolen lands were returned to the Welsh of Senghenydd. After that, the Normans did not feel so safe in their castle strongholds.

Many of today's Cardiff Welsh enjoy contemporary Welsh entertainment at a nightclub called **Clwb Ifor Bach** in Womamby Street, which is located right opposite the Cardiff Castle walls that the little Senghenydd hero climbed nearly nine hundred years ago!

Robert the Consul died in 1147 and the de Clare family succeeded through marriage after Robert's son William died without heir. The most formidable de Clare was red-headed Gilbert the Red who built Caerphilly castle – twice. The first castle was destroyed by the Welsh prince Llywelyn ap Gruffudd; the second, built in 1271, is a huge fortification with a double moat, famous today for its leaning tower. Gilbert then strengthened Cardiff Castle with a massive forebuilding on the southern side of the Keep with a thick wall extending almost to the South Gate which he reinforced and then built the Black Tower. A steep climb takes one up the (restored) steps of the forebuilding to the battlements of the Keep giving a fine view of the castle and its surroundings.

The lordship of Cardiff Castle passed to the Despenser family in 1306 which held it for one hundred years. Grasping and tyrannical, they were hated by English and Welsh alike. In 1318 the younger Hugh, Lord Despenser ignited a revolt by Prince Llywelyn Bren of the Glamorgan lowlands. The Welsh armies captured and destroyed many Norman castles, but when his men were outnumbered and surrounded, Llywelyn Bren surrendered his own life into the hands of the Despenser Lord. Immediately it was ordered that Llywelyn be shamefully dragged through the streets of Cardiff, hung, drawn and quartered, later announced to be an illegal execution. Despenser was said to have had a gay relationship with Edward II and they were certainly close friends but when Despenser's plotting and manipulation of the king eventually resulted in a conviction for treachery, he suffered a similar fate: he is depicted in a contemporary painting tied to a ladder, his genitals cut off, his entrails removed and burnt before his eyes. Finally he was beheaded and his head sent to London to be displayed outside the Tower.

The town of Cardiff grew beside the castle. It has been calculated that by the end of the 12th century the town had about two thousand inhabitants, making it the largest town in Wales. It continued to prosper until 1349 with the first outbreak of the plague which swept across England and Wales, seemingly carried to Europe by rats on ships from the Far East. Half to one third of the population died, leaving Cardiff with about fifteen hundred people. Houses and farms in town and country stood empty, animals wandered untended, there was starvation and looting.

At the turn of the century disaster struck the Norman overlords again. Owain Glyndŵr (1359-1415), a Marcher lord with Welsh royal blood in his veins, was declared Prince of Wales by 300 of his followers and later by a full Welsh Parliament, and led the Welsh into a War of Independence against the English in 1400. The whole of Wales rallied to the national cause and his armies marched across the country, attacking and burning Norman strongholds. After taking Harlech and Aberystwyth castles, Glyndŵr reached Cardiff by 1404. By the next year he had become Wales' national leader with visions of independent statehood and a parliament in Machynlleth where the ancient building which is thought to have served as his parliament house can be seen. Entering Cardiff through the West Gate he set fire to the town which was virtually destroyed. Wales was left in a parlous state when the royal armies ordered from London entered Wales searching for Glyndŵr and his followers. Wales was almost destroyed by the conflict, with tenants dispersed, manor houses plundered and towns in ruins but Glyndŵr was never caught or betrayed. His 15 year rebellion was the longest in the history of the British Empire. It is estimated that Wales – and Cardiff – took a hundred years to recover from the rebellion and the revenge wreaked upon it by the Normans.

Aged sixteen, Henry of Monmouth,

Shakespeare's swashbuckling Prince Hal of *King Henry IV Parts 1 and 2*, was sent to lead a force against Owain Glyndŵr. Later he returned to England to help his father fight Harry Hotspur at the Battle of Shrewsbury. When Prince Hal ascended the English throne in 1413, becoming Henry IV, he set about resolving the 'Welsh situation' by trying to reconcile Glyndŵr's supporters and rewarding those who had remained loyal to the crown. He was popular among some of the gentry in spite of continuing taxation and the sale of pardons, and Welsh veterans were recruited to fight in the French wars.

In 1414 Richard Beauchamp, Lord Abergavenny, succeeded to the lordship of Cardiff Castle through marriage to eleven-year-old Isabel, Richard Despenser's sister. Widowed after eight years, she married another Beauchamp, Richard, Earl of Warwick, in 1423. He built the Great Hall of the castle and the Lodgings or domestic block and the Octagon or Beauchamp Tower. When Henry, last in the line of male Beauchamp Warwicks, died the inheritance passed through marriage to Richard Neville, the eldest son of the Earl of Salisbury who became known as Warwick the Kingmaker because of his wily meddling in the politics of the Wars of the Roses. Henry Tudor – Henry VII – plucked Richard III's crown from a bush on Bosworth battlefield in 1485 and placing it on his head said in Shakespeare's words '*We will unite the white rose with the red*'. Henry Tudor was descended from the Tudors, an Anglesey family of Welsh noblemen, claiming royal descent from his grandmother, Henry V's widow, Catherine. Catherine and Owain Tudor had two sons,

Owain Glyndŵr's Parliament House at Machynlleth, Powys c.1402. Lord David Davies of Llandinam built the half-timbered house when in 1911 when the Parliament House was being restored.

Edmund and Jasper. Edmund died in 1456, two months before the birth of his son Henry Tudor who then lived under the guardianship of his uncle Jasper. For the boy's safety during the protectorship and reign of Richard III, Jasper and his nephew Henry had fled to France where they enlisted French support. In 1485 they had landed at Dale (some say at Milford Haven) in Pembrokeshire to claim the throne for young Henry. As they travelled to Bosworth they amassed an army of around 5,000 soldiers and were joined by the forces of Sir William Stanley, Justice of North Wales, who turned the Battle of Bosworth in their favour. Thus a Welsh monarch ascended the throne of England, receiving the allegiance of the people of Wales and founding the royal dynasty of the Tudors. One of Henry's first actions was to confiscate the marcher lordship of Glamorgan and Cardiff Castle from the Nevilles and grant them to his uncle Jasper. When Jasper died nine years later they reverted to the crown.

The tower of the Church of St John the

The Tower of St John's c.1473, an enduring landmark of Cardiff, appear in many historic drawings and paintings.

Baptist dates from *c.*1473 and is likely to have been built by master mason William Hart of Bristol. The tower is the enduring landmark of Cardiff, surviving across the centuries, beloved of its citizens: it appears in early drawings and watercolours of the town behind crumbling castle walls, grazing cows and the flooded river Taff. 19th century photographs show it dominating streets bustling with horse-drawn vehicles, pedestrians and trams. It was there in wartime, protected by barrage balloons. It is still the heart of Cardiff, tall and slender, decorated with that lacy pattern of pinnacles, pierced battlements and crockets (*carvings of unfurling leaves*). I have spent many happy hours sketching it from different viewpoints but always focussing on the intricate (and difficult!) top of the tower. The graveyard was to the south west, roughly as it is today, but surrounded by a wall. Beyond the graveyard were burgages (*plots with dwellings and gardens*) and open spaces separated by *hays* or hedges where flax, fruit and other crops were grown and after which The Hayes of today is named. In 1542 a survey showed that there were 370 burgages. Historian John Leland had

A roundel from the late medieval natural oak parclose screen enclosing the tomb of the Herbert brothers.

before 1542 written in his '*Itinerary*' that Cardiff was '*the fairest town in Wales*' that it had five gates and the circumference of the walls measured a mile. Today blue plaques mark some parts of the walls and gates of the old town: **East Gate's** plaque is on the corner of Greyfriars and Queen Street and there are sections of the wall in the Kingsway flower bed and up the alley between One Kingsway and the Northgate Building; **West Gate** is in the Castle walls; **North Gate** or Senghenydd Gate was in Kingsway; **South Gate** was on the site of the Central Hotel, St Mary Street. This was how central Cardiff remained, little changed, until the 18th century, as did the rest of the town.

3. Henry VIII to Elizabeth I

The Act of Union, the Reformation, St Fagans Castle, a small town

Henry VIII, famously husband of five wives, succeeded to the throne in 1509. Holbein's famous portraits show him powerful and arrogant, as he wished to be seen. Another Holbein portrait is of Jane Seymour who died giving birth to the future Edward VI and another shows baby Edward holding his golden rattle, wearing a gorgeous red and gold doublet, a tiny feathered hat on his head in imitation of his father. There is certainly a strong family likeness. Henry VIII's rule was marked by wars against France and Scotland and he needed more money. He saw that the church was very rich with many monasteries, ripe for plundering so the Lord Chancellor Thomas Cromwell began carrying out the tenets of the Dissolution of the Monasteries (1536). Blackfriars and Greyfriars in Cardiff were dissolved, but having only fifteen friars between them they were already in serious decline. The foundations of Blackfriars remain in Bute Park, excavated by the 3rd Marquess of Bute in c.1892. The ruins of Greyfriars were bought by Sir George Herbert (a distant relative of the Herberts of Cardiff Castle p. 21 & 23)) who had built a fine stone house on the site by 1578.

Greyfriars House fell into disuse, eventually becoming a romantic ruin by the 18th century. These ruins survived in a

remnant of the graveyard until 1967 when they were wrongfully demolished, obliterating a picturesque historic site that formed a link between the Civic Centre and the town and spoiling the scale and setting of nearby buildings. The large office block, the **Capital Tower** that replaced it, has not improved with age.

The Act of Union between England and Wales (1536) extended the English system of administration and justice into Wales when Cardiff became the county town of Glamorgan. Justice was administered and elections for Glamorgan Members of Parliament were held in the Shire Hall which was in the outer ward of the castle, east of Gilbert the Red's dividing wall (p. 14).

The Six Articles of Faith were placed on the Statute Book in 1539: '*pain of death by way of burning*' and confiscation of goods was the punishment for those who did not accept the Catholic doctrine of Transubstantiation outlined in the First Article. Thomas Capper, a Cardiff citizen who could not accept the First Article, was burnt at the stake for heresy after

Ruined Greyfriars House, a photograph taken in c.1955.

imprisonment for one hundred and thirty days in the '*cwchmoel*' or '*cochmoil*', the prison section of the Guildhall in High Street. Capper is the only Cardiffian recorded as being burnt for heresy at that time, but surely there would have been others.

Twelve-year-old Edward VI ascended the throne in 1547 and four years later made his guardian Sir William Herbert, 1st Earl of Pembroke and brother-in-law of Henry VIII's widow Catherine Parr, Baron of Cardiff Castle. Sir William altered the Lodgings and spent lavishly on new furnishings such as carpets, tapestries and leather hangings together with velvet, silk and satin curtains; some of these and others of the period can be seen in the castle.

Mary, Henry VIII's daughter by Catherine of Aragon, seized the throne after young Edward's death in 1553 and immediately executed Lady Jane Grey, the 'Nine Days Queen' for treason. She abolished the two books of Common Prayer, reinstated the Mass, celibate clergy and holy days. Thomas Cranmer, writer of anti-Catholic liturgical documents and the two books of Common Prayer, was burnt for heresy in 1556. Three hundred protestants are recorded as having been burnt at the stake for heresy during her reign. One was Welshman Rawlins White, a Cardiff fisherman with a half-burgage near Quay Street and five henges or weirs along the Taff estuary and Roath sea bank where he spread his nets to trap fish on the tide. He was illiterate but memorised large parts of the Bible read to him by his son and took to preaching his own versions of theology around Cardiff. He was eventually arrested in 1555 and taken to Bishop Kitchin of Llandaff's residence at Mathern where the Bishop patiently tried to persuade him to recant his protestant beliefs, ordering a Mass to be said for him, to no avail. He was therefore imprisoned in the cochmoil from where he was to be taken out to be burned but, as there was no writ to authorise the burning, one was hastily obtained from London. Rawlins White died in the flames near St John's. A bronze plaque commemorating him, removed from Bethany Baptist Chapel in Wharton Street when it was demolished, can be seen in the ground floor of Howell's store.

The reign of Elizabeth I (1558-1603), sometimes spoken of as a brief Golden Age, brought relative peace to England and Wales. There was little change in Cardiff which remained an insignificant town. It should have developed into a prosperous maritime and commercial centre when in 1557 it was made into one of the head ports of Wales bringing the right to collect customs duties. But Cardiff had become notorious as the headquarters of a gang of pirates who operated along the Bristol Channel and terrorised the townsfolk. At least once they were brazen enough to bring a captive Spanish ship into Cardiff itself. Things had improved by *c.*1580, because Rice Merrick, Clerk of the Peace for Glamorgan and a leading historian, was

The Herbert brothers on their tomb in the Lady Chapel of St John's.

able to write of Cardiff that '*within these Walles is little or no vacant or waste ground saving for gardens and these very small it is so well replenished with buildings*'. Some wealthy families maintained properties in the town, such as Sir William Herbert and his brother Sir John of Greyfriars. Both were Mayors and Constables of Cardiff, but Sir John had an even more distinguished career as Chief Secretary to Elizabeth I and then James I, becoming Ambassador to Denmark, Holland and France. The brothers are buried in the Lady Chapel of St John's Church.

Nothing remains of the other dwellings of central Cardiff so one must imagine the half-timbered houses we associate with the Elizabethan period alongside stone buildings and the huts of the poor, unlit muddy roads and lanes, dogs and pigs scavenging from piles of dung and other refuse lying round. Wealthy families had houses and estates in the Vale of Glamorgan.

One such house, **St Fagans Castle**, dates from the Norman period but was ruinous after a chequered history of about four hundred years. By 1580 a '*faire house within the old walls of a castle called St Faggins*'[2] had been built in the medieval ruins by Dr John Gibbon of Pentrebane as the large many-gabled mansion we see today. Through marriage the mansion passed into the hands of other notable families including Sir Richard Lewis of the Van, Caerphilly, and Other Windsor, 3rd Earl of Plymouth and 9th Baron Windsor in 1730; it remained in the possession of the Plymouth family until 1947.

St Fagans Castle went through further periods of decline, falling into disrepair by the first half of the 19th century. Some parts were taken over by the locals – it is recorded that in 1847 Sunday and day schools were held in the castle '*which is not occupied at present except by the schoolmaster and his family*'[2] and other rooms were occupied by villagers. Some restoration was carried out late in the 19th century and in 1947 the Earl of Plymouth gave the castle and gardens to the National Museum of Wales as a centre for the creation of a national folk museum.

Extensive refurbishment was carried out between 1981 and 1983 and since then, as furniture and fittings have been purchased or donated, the castle has been restored as a largely 17th century house. As you walk through the Hall, up the staircase, along the Long Gallery past the portraits, tapestries and furniture into the Great Chamber and bedrooms, it is easy to imagine the life that went on there. The fine kitchen is dominated by two huge open fireplaces, one with a giant spit turned by dog wheel. Hot, busy and noisy it would have been, but what delicious smells and fine meals must have been produced there!

Eighty acres of parkland now contain a wonderful collection of reconstructed buildings, following the tradition of folk museums in Scandinavia. I never tire of visiting St Fagans, sketching and painting and trying to capture the colour and details of those fascinating houses and workshops, but there is still so much to do before even starting on the recent additions! In 2014 St Fagans was transformed into **St Fagans National**

History Museum but it has never stopped farming, furnishing, and reconstructing buildings. The Vulcan Arms from Adam Street, Cardiff dismantled in 2013 and currently in storage, is one such building waiting its turn to be rebuilt.

St Fagans is open from 10am – 5pm daily.

Two re-erected buildings at St Fagans:
1. Abernodwydd Farm from Llangadfan in Montgomeryshire, 16th century, renovated in the 17th century; 2. A slate-pillared hay shed from Maentwrog in Gwynedd.

4. The Seventeenth Century

The great flood, the Battle of St Fagans, two Welsh Martyrs

The most momentous event of the 17th century was the great flood of 1607 in the Bristol Channel. There is a conflict of opinion as to whether the cause was a tsunami or a combination of bad weather with a high tide creating a storm surge but, whatever the cause, the 1607 flood is the largest natural disaster to have befallen England and Wales during the last five hundred years, seemingly even greater than the 2014 floods.

On 20th January 1607[3] *'one or more mighty hilles of water'* swept over the sea defences of the Bristol Channel *'running with a swiftness so incredible that no greyhound could have escaped before them'* flooding more than twenty parishes in the hinterlands of the Channel, sweeping all before them. Around two thousand people died, hundreds of buildings were destroyed, animals drowned and farmlands laid waste. On the Welsh side the effects were felt from Laugharne (Carmarthenshire) to Monmouth (Gwent). A contemporary writer said that *'The farmers and shepherds might behold their goodly flocks swimming on the waters dead'*[3] and Mistress Mathew of Llandaff, dwelling some four miles from the sea, was said to have lost four hundred English ewes.

It has been estimated that Cardiff took about a hundred years to recover from the 1607 flood, but John Speed's 1610 map does not seem to take much account of flood

Contemporary woodcut of the 1607 flood.

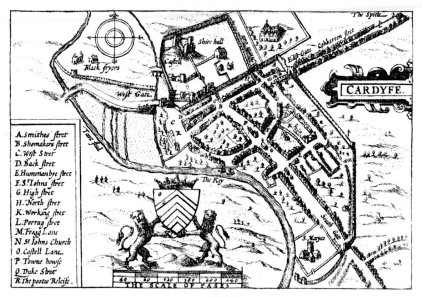

The map legend reads:

A. *Smithes ſtret*
B. *Shomakers ſtret*
C. *Weſt Stret*
D. *Back ſtret*
E. *Hummanbye ſtret*
F. *S. Iohns ſtret*
G. *High ſtret*
H. *North ſtret*
K. *Working ſtret*
L. *Porraq ſtret*
M. *Frogg Lane*
N. *St Iohns Church*
O. *Caſtell Lane*
P. *Towne houſe*
Q. *Duke Stret*
R. *The pootes Releiſe*

CARDYFE.

THE SCALE OF PASES

John Speed's 1610 Map.

damage. The map shows the Taff with a huge bend and a mill stream coming from a point above Blackweir, running along the west wall of the castle on the line of the present canal feeder and passing under the road at the West Gate. It shows trees and houses beside the mill stream on West Street, cottage industries, workshops and the town quay. Corn and fulling mills are known to have worked beside the river at least from the middle ages. John Speed's map also shows a wall or palisade and gatehouse marking the boundary of Blackfriars Farm which had an estate of about four acres, with buildings and dwellings, orchards, kitchen gardens and meadows.

Another momentous event of the 17th century was the Civil War and the **Battle of St Fagans**. On 8 May, 1648 the Roundhead (Parliamentarian) army of Oliver Cromwell defeated the Cavaliers (Royalists) supporting Charles I at the Battle of St Fagans.

The Battle of Edgehill in 1642 was the first major confrontation of the Civil War when William Herbert, Royalist MP for Cardiff, was killed. The people of Cardiff were divided in their allegiances. Sir William Herbert, Lord of Cardiff Castle, was a Parliamentarian so the King gained little Royalist support when he visited Cardiff in 1645. Major General Colonel Rowland Laugharne, a Parliamentarian, took Cardiff town and castle at the Battle of the Heath when some two hundred and fifty Royalists were killed. Col. Laugharne, who had won other victories in Wales, changed sides and later took command of the Royalists. Colonel Thomas Horton led a Parliamentarian force of three thousand men (one regiment of foot and two of horse) to take up positions around the Pentrebane ridge. Col. Laugharne's Royalist force consisted of more than eight thousand foot with about 500 horse and both sides would have been armed with muskets, pikes and swords.

Early in the morning of May 8th 1648, the Royalists made a surprise attack on the

St Fagans Castle (c.1560-1580) the west elevation overlooking the Italian Garden.

Parliamentarians who were quartered in and around St Fagans, hoping to trap them in the village and surroundings. Battle continued throughout the day in fields and lanes west of St Fagans and ended in victory for the Parliamentarians. How frightening to be walking peacefully along a lane and to be suddenly confronted by men in what we think of as picturesque costumes battling with swords or charging with pikes on horseback! It was a disaster for the Royalists. The number of casualties was not recorded except to say that no officers were killed or wounded although two suffered shots into their hats. Four officers were executed and two hundred and forty men sent to Barbados. Four thousand more were disarmed and sent home. Cromwell arrived eight days later.

According to an eye-witness, in that same year, when Charles I was beheaded outside his Banqueting House in Whitehall, London *'there was such a groan by the thousands then present as I never heard before, and desire that I may never hear again'*[4].

The people of Cardiff were accustomed to the proselytising and preaching of the Puritans and their disapproval of dancing,

St Fagans Castle (c.1560-1580), was built on the ruins of a medieval fort. This is the south elevation, approached through the medieval walls.

games, bright clothes and many other harmless pleasures especially on Sundays, so Cromwell's repressions came as no surprise. He tolerated the various Nonconformist denominations, but the Books of Common Prayer were banned and Roman Catholicism outlawed. Churches were desecrated, lay people persecuted while torture and death was the fate of priests celebrating Mass. Maypoles were cut down and the celebration of feast days abolished although Christmas had already been outlawed. Cardiff kept its Protestants. One, William Wroth, Rector of Llanvaches, became famous for his preaching. He lost his living because he no longer held Anglican beliefs and led the first gathered church of Nonconformists in Wales according to the New England pattern (that is Congregationalist) which met at Llanvaches. The chapel, now the United Reformed Church, Llanvaches, originally dating from 1639, stands beside the A48 road between Chepstow and Newport. One of the earliest Quaker Meetings in Wales was established in Cardiff and Friends now meet in the former vicarage of St John's in Charles Street.

Catholic Charles ll brought back a degree of religious toleration when he ascended the throne in 1660, but fear of Catholics and Catholic countries was embedded in the national psyche. Manipulating this fear, the renegade priest Titus Oates fabricated a story of a Jesuit plot to assassinate the king resulting in a wave of Catholic persecution of the Jesuits in particular.

In 1679 two Welsh priests were executed in Cardiff: one, Philip Evans a Jesuit Priest, was arrested at Sker House near Port Talbot and imprisoned for five months in Cardiff Castle. Another was John Lloyd, a Brecon man, who exercised his ministry for twenty years before being arrested and charged with saying Mass at Llantilio and Penrhos (Monmouthshire) and was imprisoned with Philip Evans. They were tried together, found guilty of being priests and condemned to the awful death of hanging, drawing and quartering. They died at Gallows Field on 22nd July, 1679. Gallows Field was on the junction of Albany, City, Richmond, Crwys Roads and Mackintosh Place, Roath. The priests were canonised by Pope John Paul Vl in 1970 as two of the Forty Martyrs of England and Wales.

The 2nd Earl of Pembroke and Lord of

Cardiff Castle lived in it, but the 3rd and 4th Earls (1601-50), patrons of Shakespeare, were enticed away to the pleasures of London and spent more time at Wilton, their splendid house and park near Salisbury. Neglected, Cardiff Castle fell into decay and as the castle was a major source of employment and local trading the town stagnated. The 1607 flood, the Civil War and not being on one of the major drovers' roads linking Wales to London and other English markets all

Sker House near Port Talbot (in 1977) was built by the Catholic Turbervilles in this isolated spot. It's certainly romantic, used by R.D. Blackmore in his novel 'The Maid of Sker'. Despite being inhabited until 1977 it was very neglected but happily was restored and occupied in 2012.

contributed to its decline; on the other hand Brecon, Carmarthen and Cowbridge, being on these roads, thrived.

5. Cardiff and Iron Making: the Eighteenth Century

Ironmasters, the Glamorganshire Canal, Cardiff, town and Castle, the 1st Marquess of Bute

The 18th century saw the birth of Cardiff's rise to greatness with the growth of iron making in Glamorganshire. Iron making was already going on in South Wales during earlier centuries but was spurred on in the 17th century when English iron-masters were prevented from taking further timber from Sussex woodlands because it was needed to build ships for the Spanish wars. As timber was essential to make charcoal for iron smelting when coal was not available, some ironmasters came to Welsh forests, so during the 16th century blast furnaces and forges appeared near Cardiff at Tongwynlais and Pentyrch. There were also successful works in the Wye Valley, especially at Tintern and Pontypool. Iron was first taken by canal to Newport and then shipped to ports such as Bridgewater, Bristol, London and the Dutch port of Flushing.

Abraham Darby revolutionised the process of iron making in 1709 by successfully smelting iron ore with coke at Coalbrookdale in Shropshire, but it was not until the mid 18th century that English ironmasters saw that coking coal and iron stone were conveniently close together in the Merthyr Tydfil area. Limestone, used as a flux during smelting, and stone for building furnaces could be quarried nearby. Many large and small iron works sprang up around Merthyr within a generation.

The four largest ironworks at Merthyr were set up by English entrepreneurs. They were: Cyfarthfa, owned by the Crawshays; the Plymouth Iron Company owned by the Earl of Plymouth; the Penydarren Ironworks owned by Samuel Homfray; and Dowlais owned by Sir Josiah John Guest. Of these, perhaps the Crawshays and the Guests are the most well-known.

Richard Crawshay, son of a Yorkshire farmer, left home for London when he was

sixteen and started working life selling flat irons in an iron warehouse, eventually buying the business and becoming a successful iron merchant. Seeking to invest his profits, he acquired a cannon-boring business at Cyfarthfa (on the outskirts of Merthyr), then leased and bought Cyfarthfa Iron Works in 1768. Hard and imperious, Richard Crawshay known as 'The Tyrant', developed Cyfarthfa into the largest iron-making business in South

Cyfarthfa Castle 1824-5 designed by Robert Lugar who had instructions not to exceed a budget of £30,000.

Wales. When he died his estate was worth £1.5 million which was divided between his son William, his son-in-law and his nephew. By 1820 William Crawshay had turned Cyfarthfa into the largest ironworks in the world employing about 1,500 people.

Sir Josiah John Guest 1785-1852.

Lady Charlotte Guest 1812-1895.

Cyfarthfa Castle is now the excellent **Merthyr Tydfil Museum**, which also holds an important collection of work by Merthyr artist Penry Williams who was supported by Crawshay. After study at the Royal Academy in London he went to Italy and developed his career, specialising in Italian subjects. Some ironworkers' cottages have been re-erected at St Fagans National History Museum. Six out of seven ruined furnaces in the valley opposite the Castle survive and can be explored (with care!) on foot. The birthplace of Sir Joseph Parry in Chapel Row in Merthyr is one of a row of ironworkers' cottages. Ynysfach Engine House Interpretation Centre on Ynysfach Road was created in the 1836 blast-engine house. Cyfarthfa Castle is open most days.

Josiah John Guest's grandfather John had come to Wales from Brosley, near Coalbrookdale. He was made manager of the Dowlais furnace in 1767 and used the latest technology of coke and steam power, rapidly increasing production to supply iron for armaments used in the American War of Independence (1775-83) and the Napoleonic Wars (1799-1815). His son Thomas was a partner in the Dowlais Iron Company and Josiah John assumed control of the works in 1805. By 1815 five blast furnaces were producing 15,600 tons

Dowlais Ironworks, George Childs 1840.

of iron annually and by the mid 1840s 10,000 people were employed at Dowlais, overtaking Cyfarthfa as the largest ironworks in the world. Dowlais was also operating rolling mills, forges and foundries. When railways began to spread across Britain and Europe, Dowlais was the leading supplier of the vast quantities of rails exported as far away as Russia and the U.S.A.

Landscapes by artists such as Penry Williams and George Childs often romanticise ironworks, giving them rural settings in the soft light of evening or rosy glow of night lit by the furnaces. Two views of Dowlais by George Childs show it in a more realistic way with men working, one showing a dramatic darkening sky and smoke blowing across the works. In reality, working conditions in all the Merthyr

Tydfil ironworks were atrocious. The iron workers lived in damp, over-crowded cottages with no running water or sanitation. Single workers took lodgings, often sleeping in relays since the furnaces worked a seven-day week, day and night. Some lived in streets or shacks whilst others might find a warm place to sleep beside the furnaces. Outbreaks of dysentery, typhoid and cholera were frequent as were child deaths from disease and malnutrition. Accidents were commonplace. Merthyr was hot and stinking in summer, cold, wet and stinking in winter, with no escape from noise, flames, smoke and dirt.

Lady Charlotte Guest assisted Sir Josiah in the business but also tried to improve conditions by doing social work including starting a school above the works stables. She commissioned Sir

1. *Guest Stables in Merthyr 1969. The upper floors were used as a school by Lady Charlotte Guest; 2. Sir Charles Barry's Central School (1855).*

Charles Barry, architect of the Houses of Parliament, to design a new school, opened 1855 in memory of her husband, who died in 1852 and the Guest Memorial Reading Room & Library (1863). Lady Charlotte bore ten children and kept a diary describing in vivid detail the family's life. Incredibly, alongside all this she learnt Welsh, enabling herself to make the first translation of the 'Mabinogion' (*an ancient collection of Welsh stories*) into English. It is still a respected standard work.

In 1891 Dowlais Ironworks made a partial move to Cardiff where it continued to operate and eventually merged to become part of Guest, Keen & Nettlefold in 1900.

By the late 1700s, the difficulty and time taken to transport iron to Cardiff down rough tortuous roads (the present A4054 and A470) to small wharves on the Taff was so great that the ironmasters, led by Crawshay, engaged Thomas Dadford, a pupil of the famous canal engineer James Brindley, to design the Glamorganshire Canal. It opened in stages: the first connecting Merthyr to Pontypridd opened in 1792; the second stage opened in 1794 to

a canal basin and lock at present day East and West Canal Wharves in Cardiff; and finally to a sea lock in the Taff estuary, celebrated in style with a naval procession and the firing of guns in 1798. Now one horse could draw twenty-five tons of iron or coal in canal barges instead of four horses or mules taking just two tons.

At the opening of the 18th century Cardiff was still a small town, ready for expansion and in contemporary paintings it looks picturesque. One can imagine the groups of burgages with their gardens and orchards, wandering hens and pigs, horses and carts, but the town was in a sorry state. Well into the 18th century the streets were unpaved and unlit, water had to be fetched from the river or a few town wells. There was no real sanitation and foul dung heaps stank by St John's and in St Mary Street. Butchers threw revolting offal into the streets from slaughter sheds in their premises. There was amusement for those who liked to watch public hangings outside the cochmoel or at Gallows Field. You could see bull baiting in Crokerton (or Crokerherbtown, now Queen Street) and dog or cock fights. Drunkenness was endemic with a tavern for every 27 males. The drinking, feuding and brawling calls to mind a miniature version of Hogarth's engravings of London.

St John's was dilapidated, damaged by the 1607 flood and another violent storm in 1674 and had to be repaired. A complete overhaul of the roof, re-paving of the floor with stone brought by boat from Lavernock near Penarth and the casting of new bells was commenced in 1708 and a Harris organ was installed. Trees were lopped and new ones planted in St John's Square. Pest controls were introduced with a tariff payable to people who caught pests such as badgers, stoats, weasels, pole cats and hedgehogs: the rate for a dead pole cat was 4d, 2d for a hedgehog[5]. Trade was increasing too and in 1760 the wall of the town quay on the Taff was built up to handle extra shipping. By 1768 streets were being paved, cleaned and lit and action taken against those who allowed their pigs to roam or were responsible for refuse and dung heaps.

Cardiff Castle passed to the Windsor family through the marriage of Charlotte, daughter of the 7th Earl of Pembroke, to the 1st Viscount Windsor. John, Lord Mount Stuart married Charlotte Jane, granddaughter of the 1st Viscount Windsor, and was made Baron of Cardiff

Castle; in 1766 he became the 1st Marquess of Bute. Bute wealth was further increased when Charlotte Jane died and he married a second heiress, Fanny Coutts of the banking family. The 1st Marquess's main business interests were directed to enlarging the family's Glamorgan estates, spending at least £30,000 on buying lands which included Adamsdown, Maendy, the Friars estate encompassing Cathays, most of Cogan and Leckwith, and the Great Heath.

Cardiff in the 19th century showing the castle and St John's.

The 1st Marquess engaged the well-known architect Robert Adam to prepare plans for modernising the Lodgings, but they were never carried out and it was Henry Holland, architect son-in-law of 'Capability' Brown, who carried out extensive alterations after 1776. He added the Drawing Room with its odd mixture of classical and Gothic windows and the Bute Tower. Capability Brown carried out the Marquess's remodelling of the bailey which by then contained some domestic buildings and gardens, a chapel and the Shire Hall, all of which he cleared away whilst retaining the remains of the Forebuilding walls from the Keep to the Black Tower. Did he overdo the clearance? I think so, as did others at the time. He also had the trees which had grown on the motte removed, ivy stripped from the Keep, the moat filled in and the grounds landscaped.

6. Coal: The Nineteenth Century

Coal mining remained secondary to iron making in South Wales until *c*.1824, but times had begun to change. Some fifty years earlier James Watt had pioneered the harnessing of steam power to stationery engines and, as smelting with coke had revolutionised iron making, so did the adaptation of steam power to stationery engines dramatically change coal mining. Until then coal had been mined mainly from outcrops and seams near the surface, but the use of steam-powered pumping engines and other mining appliances greatly improved the drainage and ventilation of deep mines where there was more, better quality coal. Mining for the best quality steam coal therefore became the most important industry of the South Wales Valleys.

A number of people have been credited with being the first to mine steam coal in Glamorganshire, but it seems the honour must go to Robert Thomas of Waun Wyllt near Abercanaid who, in 1824, acquired a lease from ironmaster the Earl of Plymouth to mine coal and iron stone for sale to the public. Thomas opened a colliery, constructed a tram road to the Glamorganshire Canal near Glyndyrys, and set up a coal yard at the Iron Bridge in Merthyr to supply coal to local residents. When he died his widow Mrs Lucy Thomas continued the business and after many tribulations created a link with Cardiff ship owner George Insole. She was such a successful business woman that she was named '*Mother of the Steam Coal Trade*.'[6]

From these modest beginnings the Glamorganshire Valleys were transformed into a vast coalfield with pits along the Taff and Cynon valleys, to be followed by more pits in the Rhondda Fach, Rhondda Fawr, Aberdare and other valleys. By 1860 the output of the Glamorganshire coalfield had reached over 10 million tons. This was doubled twenty years later and by 1913 the staggering total of 57 million tons of coal was being produced.

One of the most successful coal owners was David Davies of Llandinam in Montgomeryshire whose granddaughters Margaret and Gwendoline used his wealth to patronise the arts. (page 113) In 1866 he

Merthyr Vale Colliery in 1978.

opened the Maindy and Parc pits and then pits in the Garw and Ogwr valleys. He turned his mining operations into the huge Ocean Coal Co. Ltd. which, by 1890, had become the largest coal producer in South Wales. Finding that Cardiff Docks and the Taff Vale Railway (designed by I.K. Brunel and opened in 1855) were unable to deal with such huge quantities of coal, he built a railway line from a junction at Hafod near Pontypridd to connect with new docks he built at Barry.

Coal production declined after the 1914-18 War. It continued to decline during the 1920s due to the General Strike and Depression of those years, which created an inability to compete with cheaper imports from Spain and South America and the increasing use of oil. There was a brief revival during the 1939-45 War but in 1947 pit closures began and continued until 1994 with the closure of Tower Colliery at Hirwaun, the last deep mine in South Wales. Tower Colliery miners made a buyout bid for the colliery and 200 miners became shareholders in the new company which continued operations until 2000.

The story of the Glamorganshire Valleys is told at the former Lewis Merthyr Colliery (1870s), which has become the **Rhondda Heritage Park** at Trehafod near Pontypridd. The National Coal Museum is at Blaenavon in Monmouthshire.

Images of Welsh valley towns overshadowed by dark slag tips, steep mountain sides and gaunt head frames are inextricably linked to Cardiff's history. Such scenes make wonderful subjects full of meaning but the demands of a young family sadly prevented me from travelling round the Valleys with my sketch book. Other artists such as Ernest Zobole, John Petts, Colin Jones, Joseph Herman and Valerie Ganz movingly painted and drew miners and their surroundings. Life is also hauntingly described by Richard Llewellyn in his novel *How Green Was my Valley* and

1. *A headframe at Deep Navigation Colliery, Treharris drawn in 1992 during demolition;*
2. *Abercynon with its Workingmen's Institute in 1978; 3. top: Pen-y-Graig Rhondda Fawr, bottom: Ty Mawr Colliery.*

now runs along the opposite side of the valley to the winding A4054, halving the journey to Cardiff.

The millions of tons of steam coal pouring down to Cardiff from those Valleys during the mid to late 19th century turned the market-sized town into a wealthy metropolis and a city by 1905. Without the creation of the docks by the Butes, none of this would have happened.

other writers such as Alexander Cordell.

Rows of terraced houses still line the valley sides. Some chapels and churches, pubs and Workingmen's institutes remain but there are few of the solid stone-built engine houses, often with iron framed 'Georgian' windows, outlined in brick. No headframes, workshops, coal heaps, railway lines and trucks or other essential mining equipment. Dwindling memories of that once great coal mining era remain although Valley homes are now overshadowed not by dark tips but by green hillsides. The Glamorganshire Canal is all but filled in but Merthyr Tydfil and the Valleys are still connected to Cardiff by Brunel's Taff Vale Railway. The A 470 road

PEN-Y-GRAIG
RHONDDA FAWR

TY MAWR COLL⸍
HETTY SHAFT⸍

WEDNESDAY
JULY 12TH

7. The Docks

The 2nd Marquess of Bute, Tiger Bay, Mount Stuart Square

Imagine wetlands and marsh instead of Cardiff Bay. Little to be seen except the sky and banks of tufted grass and mud interwoven by rivulets and pools, the whole submerged when the tide flows in. There are foreshore and marsh birds, gulls circling overhead, flocks of migrating geese in the spring and autumn. Cattle, sheep and horses graze at low tide. The rivers Taff and Ely flow into the bay with wooden quays on their banks to deal with catches of fish and goods being traded to and fro along the coast or across the Bristol Channel. Boats wait in Penarth Roads, sheltering from prevailing westerlies in the lee of Penarth Head, to come in or go out on the next tide, St Augustine's Church tower on Penarth Head then, as now, an important landmark for sailors.

John Crichton Stuart, 2nd Marquess of Bute (1793-1848) began expanding Cardiff docks in the mid 19th century. He spent little time in Cardiff, becoming something of a recluse, and managing his widespread estates by letter to his many agents from Mountstuart House on the Isle of Bute. He began mining for coal at Rhigos and elsewhere on his Glamorgan estate and began to expand the docks.

Risking the fortune he had inherited from his father the 1st Marquess of Bute (p.

39) the 2nd Marquess began constructing docks to export the iron and coal coming down in increasing quantities from Merthyr Tydfil and the Valleys. The first, Bute West Dock (1839) had almost bankrupted him and was only just beginning to show a profit when he died in 1848 aged only fifty-one. The stress caused by the construction of Bute West Dock and financial difficulties alongside efforts to manage his widely spread estates, serious myopia and an inability to delegate, seem to have contributed to his early death. Nevertheless, his son John Patrick Crichton, then aged only six months, was said to be the richest baby in the world. As the owner of much Cardiff land the 2nd Marquess laid out roads such as Bute Street, designated open spaces as parks, gave money for schools and churches and was also remembered for acts of kindness to individual citizens in need. "Weep sons of Cambria" wrote contemporary historian

1. *Photograph of Cardiff Docks in the 19th century; 2. Raeburn's portrait of John Crichton Stuart, 2nd Marquess of Bute, which shows an attractive large-eyed curly-haired young man. It seemed that on first meeting he could be dour and withdrawn.*

George Clarke and he was called the Creator of Modern Cardiff.

Until young John Patrick Crichton attained his majority, the Bute Estate was managed by Trustees who built two further docks. In the space of some forty years the Trustees and the 3rd Marquess of Bute (as John Patrick Crichton became in 1868) constructed further docks and made Cardiff the largest coal exporting port in the world. The new docks were connected to the Bristol Channel by lock gates so that loading need never cease.

Faded sepia lends charm to 19th and early 20th century photographs but the reality must have been a hell of clanging

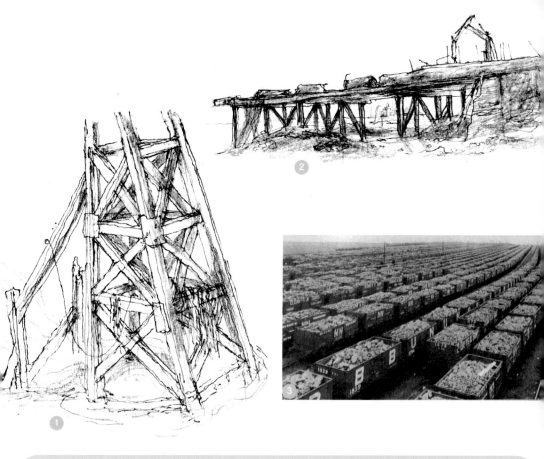

1. A 'dolphin' in Cardiff Bay. The sloping sides of these loading platforms supported ships at low tide so that loading could continue round the clock; 2. One of the last coal loading platforms; 3. Historic photo of the serried ranks of coal wagons waiting shipment.

metal, crashing coal, freezing rain and snow, dust and black mud. Monstrous steam locomotives shunting coal wagons round the docks added to the drama of the scene with heaps of coal everywhere. Stacks of pit props and piles of stone waited to be taken up by canal or railway to the coal-field. Pit props and stone used in building were often the ballast in returning empty coal ships.

Tiger Bay was made famous by the 1958 film of that name with John Mills and his daughter Hayley. One of her young fellow actors, docklands historian and writer Neil Sinclair, describes it in his book *The Tiger Bay Story* as an urban village, a place of hardship but ethnic harmony, a closely knit warm community quite separate from 'up town' which was rarely visited. He thinks the name came from a seamen's song with a line referring to old Tiger Bay, or from Portuguese sailors who claimed that sailing into the choppy waters of the bay was like entering '*Una bahia de los tigres*'.

With the growth of the docks an international community of ship repairers, dockers, seamen, trades people, publicans, boarding house and brothel keepers established itself in Butetown. It was a shifting, vibrant mix of nationalities

The 1958 film poster of the film 'Tiger Bay'.

including Greeks, Norwegians, Irish, English, Portuguese and Maltese as well as the Welsh, all living and lodging together in crowded streets. Cardiff was the first British port to have a settled Arab community and a mosque; it had strong links with Aden in the Yemen where British steamships stopped to refuel on their way to outposts of empire east of Suez. Yemeni seamen were often taken on

as stokers because they stood up well to the fierce heat of ships' engine rooms.

Another picture of Tiger Bay emerges from Howard Spring's complete autobiography published in 1972 where he wrote '*The whole place was a warren of seamen's boarding houses, dubious hotels, ships chandlers smelling of rope and tarpaulin ... It was a dirty, smelly, rotten and romantic district, an offence and an inspiration and I loved it*'. Neil Sinclair mentions the riots of 1919 when demobilised seamen saw their jobs threatened by 'foreign' seamen and took to the streets in violence. Police barricaded Bute Street to stop the mob charging down from St Mary Street and clashing with Butetown people. Three died and dozens were injured.

It seems that Tiger Bay's reputation for violence might partly

1. *The Norwegian Church Centre, Cardiff Bay. The reconstructed Norwegian Church, moved from its original site by Bute East Dock in 1992 (p. 63). Children's writer Roald Dahl, son of a Norwegian ship owner, spent his early life in Cardiff and is commemorated in the Church; 2. The Islamic Centre, Alice Street (1980) replaced the Islamic Centre in Maria Street; 3. Houses in Bute Esplanade.*

hopes it would have been restored. Windsor Esplanade, Windsor Terrace and Bute Esplanade was an area where ships provision and chandlers merchants, pilots and captains lived to keep an eye on the movement of shipping. Lookouts stationed in many attics would run to their masters' stores when they spied ships coming in on the tide that might need provisioning. The houses are large with gardens and a channel view and, after a period of decay, are once again desirable residences, part of the Pierhead Conservation Area.

Until the advent of the Cardiff Bay Development Corporation in 1987 the area

stem from the riots, but it is also true that the international community frequenting the many pubs, boarding houses and brothels made it a part of Cardiff to be avoided by 'up town' people.

The more affluent middle class business and trades people lived in Mount Stuart Square and Loudoun Square, the latter tragically demolished in 1960. In more conservation-minded times one between Atlantic Wharf and Lloyd George Avenue (then Collingdon Road) was an untidy, fascinating muddle of railway sidings with workshops and businesses functioning alongside derelict buildings, rubbish-strewn yards and heaps of rubble.

A building in Collingdon Road was divided into a ramshackle collection of artists' studios at affordable rents by plasterboard partitions and acted as the headquarters of the Association of Artists & Designers in Wales. I had a small space with an all-important window for daylight, heated like everyone else's studio with a smelly and potentially dangerous oil heater. Artists such as Sally Moore, Tony Goble, Terry Chinn, William Brown, Lachrimosa and Adrian Metcalf were busy making art there, beginning their artistic careers.

It is interesting to look back at sketches and photographs, done when I was in a feverish hurry to record what I could of the scene before redevelopment destroyed it all. One of the most exciting – and upsetting – times was in the 1980s when I went into the Tubal Cain foundry on Tyndall Street to sketch the ancient craft of iron casting. The foundry had been working on that site since 1872, pouring

Studies of Tubal Cain Foundry.

molten iron into shapes made by wooden moulds pressed into damp sand, producing such essentials as ships' propellers and anchors, window frames, railings and gates, balconies, baths,

lavatory cisterns, boot scrapers, tools and an infinite variety of useful and ornamental articles.

Cast iron was used to stunning effect by Joseph Paxton who combined it with glass to create the 1851 Great Exhibition hall, and by Decimus Burton to construct the wonderful glass houses at Kew. There are few historic glass houses in Wales, but we have plenty of chapels whose roofs and galleries are supported by cast iron columns ornamented with leafy capitals and decorative balconies: Tabernacle in The Hayes, Conway Road Methodist Chapel in Canton and Tabernacle, Pen-y-Waun Road, Roath Park have fine examples. Houses have a variety of cast iron porches as can be seen in Kimberley and Aymsebury Roads, Penylan.

After this digression into the 1980s it is time to return to today's Butetown and Mount Stuart Square at the southern end of Bute Street.

Mount Stuart Square was the commercial heart of the docks, named after the Butes' Scottish seat on the Isle of

A resident of The Triangle, (demolished) Merthyr Tydfil sitting by her cast-iron fire and stove, precursor of the Aga.

Bute. It was conceived as part of an area intended to be a model of town planning where merchants, traders, ship owners and other businessmen would live and work. The site was originally occupied by a glassworks, part of the Guest industrial empire, and existed because of the proximity of silica sand brought down the Glamorganshire Canal. The canal has been filled in for many years and is marked by a longitudinal park and commemorative gates on James Street.

The 2nd Marquess of Bute died before work on Mount Stuart Square began, so it fell to the Trustees of the Bute Estate, acting on behalf of young John Patrick Crichton until he came of age, to carry out the scheme using the Estate architect Alexander Roos. When completed there was a self-contained community in the Square and adjacent streets which had three chapels, shops, pubs, a church, a school and a town garden in the centre. Some of the earliest surviving houses are Nos 33 & 34 (late 1850s) distinguished by shell reliefs on the first floor. The ground floor rooms of the houses were often used as offices, with the dining room and kitchen to the rear, a privy and wash house in the yard and the parlour and bedrooms upstairs. The flats in the north-west corner (2005-06) replaced the Imperial, a large classical-style hotel.

Mount Stuart Square throbbed with commercial and everyday life. Docksmen carried on their businesses showing the latest news of prices and shipping movements on slates outside, or using runners who dashed from office to office and to the Pier Head where docksmen met informally. There were solicitors and accountants and banks; horse-drawn hackney cabs, carriages and delivery carts

Spiller's Warehouse (1893) was built in this strange triangular shape to fit between railway sidings and feeder canals. It was converted into flats in 1988 by AWT Architects.

filled the streets as wives, children and servants went about their daily business. West Bute Street, James Street, and Bute Street were the main shopping centres where, along with butchers, grocers, bakers and drapers there were ships chandlers and sail makers. And pubs, many pubs. The oldest, in West Bute Street, was the Bute Dock Hotel (1839) now 'Octavo'.

Mount Stuart Square changed dramatically as Cardiff became the largest coal exporting port in the world. Trading needed a proper base and the central garden of the Square was chosen as the site for a Coal Exchange (1884-8). Some residents objected but to no avail. The huge building, designed by Edwin Seward (also architect of the Old Library) in a French Renaissance style, took three years to build and was said to have cost £60,000. It opened for business in 1886. The dominant central sections of the south and east elevations are composed of richly decorated windows set in large arches, culminating in round and oval windows and ornamental pediments (*a triangular shape over a door or window*). Terra cotta phoenixes crouch on the ridge tiles.

Mahogany and glass screens surround the trading floor, but the heavy brackets supporting the balcony are painted plaster. The Exchange Club, to the north of the Hall, was the exclusive unofficial power base of the docks: members of the club were automatically members of the Exchange, but not vice versa. These areas are now restaurants and bars. Stained glass windows shine against dark wood and two of sailing ships can be seen on request in the serving area of the restaurant.

Two splendid lions bearing clocks showing the times of tides have been moved to the entrance lobby from their original places at one end of the Hall. The opposite end is still dominated by my favourite Cardiff clock, decorated with writhing dragons embracing the legend *'tempus fugit'*, a reminder to docksmen crowding the trading floor of the shortness of life as well as the speed of business. Very Victorian! And it was here at the turn of the 20th century that the first £1 million cheque in the world is said to have been signed.

The Exchange Hotel: south elevation above the 1979 car park entrance, built in an effort to bring the Exchange back into use as the Welsh Senedd after the first (failed) referendum for Devolution in 1979.

1. *The Coal & Shipping Hall at the opening of Seward's makeover on 20 February, 1912. Ladies watch from the new balconies;*
2. *The Trading Hall Clock.*

Mount Stuart Square deteriorated with the contraction of the docks. Some buildings were demolished, others fell into decay, but in 1981 it was declared a Conservation & Improvement Area which meant that not only were buildings protected, but that public funds could be used to finance new paving, lighting, parking provision, tree-planting and street furniture. It was hoped that a new lease of life would be given to the Square, encouraging existing businesses to stay and new ones to come. This would in turn help to secure the conservation of the many listed buildings in the Square and immediate area. It was exciting, but not always cheering, to be The Victorian Society representative on the Conservation Area Advisory Group which considered planning and listed building applications in the area. Collapses and demolition 'as a dangerous structure' still went on and not all new buildings were appropriate. The conservation area was soon expanded to include the Pier Head and Graving Docks, then Windsor

Esplanade, Windsor Terrace and Bute Esplanade.

In the early 21st century Mount Stuart Square was still a doleful sight with closed buildings and empty upper floors. The Exchange was closed, surrounded by scaffolding, and on Cardiff's 'Buildings at Risk' register. Then things started to change and eventually the building was bought from Cardiff Council and planning and listed building consents given for proposals to refurbish the Coal Exchange as a hotel by the company Signature Living. **The Exchange Hotel** opened in 2017 with parts still derelict but the ground floor and some bedrooms restored, open for business. Signature Living's aim is '*to revive a building's architecture and history to create a unique space ...*' and the company's restoration work continues at the time of writing in 2019.

There is a plan of the Square on page 167.

A *relief carving in Mount Stuart Square.*

8. Cardiff Bay

The Pierhead, Barrage, Waterfront, Millenium Centre, Senedd, Norwegian Church, Sports Village and Bute Street

The **Pierhead Building** (1896-7) stands spectacularly on the central quay side of the docks. It is the lynch pin of Cardiff Bay, its jewel in the crown; the Pierhead Chambers opposite was demolished to make way for the Welsh Industrial & Maritime Museum. Other buildings came and went too in efforts to revive Butetown and the whole run-down area, bringing it new life and a reason for being. The Pierhead Building remains, strong and bright.

The Pierhead Building was built for the Cardiff Railway Company, then taken over by Bute Docks Company whose offices had burnt down in 1892. It was designed by William Frame, William Burges' chief assistant, in brilliant red terra cotta brick, clearly influenced by Cardiff Castle and Castell Coch. Gothic turrets, chimney stacks, battlements and grotesque gargoyles come straight from Burges. The huge tower with its deeply set clock, ornamentation and elaborate doorway dominates the harbour, as it was meant to do. Inside the '*Assembly at the Pierhead*' exhibition is an opportunity to see some of the interior including the manager's office with a Burges type fireplace and a vaulted bay window giving a grand view of the bay.

This story of the docks now moves from the 19th to the 20th century. In 1977 the building of the Welsh Industrial & Maritime Museum beside the Pierhead Building heralded a change of direction away from dockland industry towards leisure and tourism. Cardiff Bay Development Corporation, based in Baltic House in Mount Stuart Square (1915 Teather & Wilson) transformed the Inner Harbour. The scheme entailed the tragic demise of the Welsh Industrial & Maritime

1. The Pierhead building (1896) designed by William Frame, Burges' chief assistant; 2. Relief panel on the Pierhead Building bearing the Bute Coat of Arms, the arms of the old borough of Cardiff and the legend 'Wrth ddŵr a thân' which means 'by water and fire'.

WRTH DDWR A THAN

Cardiff, an artist's exploration 59

Museum, its contents moved to the National Maritime Museum in Swansea or to storage at Nantgarw. It was replaced by shops, restaurants and **Roald Dahl Plass** in the oval basin.

Cardiff Bay Development Corporation was also responsible for the creation of a Barrage linking the Custom House at Penarth to Queen Alexandra headland opposite, opened in 2000. It was constructed by the joint firm of Balfour Beatty and Costain to create a freshwater lake fed by the rivers Ely and Taff. There are three lock gates letting ships in and out

1. *Cardiff Bay at low tide in 1982;*
2. *The Inner Harbour of Cardiff Bay in 2016.*

of the lake and a fish pass for breeding salmon to move from sea to fresh water in the Taff. Wetlands for birds were made further along the Bay shoreline and further east towards Newport. Ironically, in 2108, Cyfoeth Naturiol Cymru – the arm of the Senedd which protects Wales' natural resources – accepted mud from the nuclear plant at Hinkley Point, Somerset (which contained 'safe' levels of radiation) to cover these SSI tidal flats. In 2008 Penarth Marina was joined to the **Norwegian Church Arts Centre** by the **Cardiff Bay Barrage Coast Path** on Heol Porth Tiegre. This is a flat walk of about a mile, invigorating on a cold, windy day with views of the Bay and Bristol Channel. On Cargo Road adjaecnt to Heol Porth Tiegre is one of Cardiff's strangest buildings: the **BBC's Roath Lock Studios** are concealed behind a long flat dark wood facade punctured by cut out shapes over a blue wall. This was designed by '*FAT UK leader in decorated sheds*'. Television shows including 'Casualty' and 'Dr Who' are made there.

Many people were against the Barrage, fearing flooding and threats to wildlife in an area of Special Scientific Interest. I was one of them, preferring the interest and beauty of the tides coming in and out over the mud flats. At 14m the tide was the second highest in the world, only outstripped by the Bay of Fundy in Canada at 16.8m. The Cardiff tides give just two hours each side of high tide for shipping to come in and out of the docks. In the 1850s Alderman Trounce recorded that '*Oftimes two or three hundred vessels were anchored in Penarth Roads, either on steam or sail waiting their turn to come into the docks, or hoping for a fair wind to proceed on the outward voyage. I have known vessels laying there for between two and three months in winter during long periods of westerly and south westerly gales*'.

With its strong tides and treacherous currents, the Bristol Channel remains a challenge to sailors.

At low tide I was captivated by the changing colours of the mud flats, sometimes shining blue or sunset pink, sometimes just '*mud, mud, glorious mud*', other times dark and menacing in an approaching storm. I spent many hours by the Inner Harbour trying to capture it all in my sketchbooks during a happy (and sad) residency at the Welsh Industrial & Maritime Museum recording the rise and fall of greenish brown water first creeping in rivulets then swirling into pools around those evocative landing stages and 'dolphins'. I also recorded as many buildings as possible and am thankful that some have been refurbished and given a new lease of life.

The waterfront was transformed by walkways, landscaping, lighting and sculpture. Amongst the first sculptures

1. The Norwegian Church on its original site beside Bute West Dock in 1982;
2. The lightship *Helwick LV14* was built in Dartmouth and commissioned by Trinity House in 1953. She was stationed for some years in the Bristol Channel and off Rhossili on the Gower. She is now the base for the Cardiff Bay Chaplaincy Team;
3. The Custom House Waterguard jacked up for removal along Ocean Road in 2016.

were reliefs of sea life interspersed with quotations in graceful calligraphy along the curving low wall going to the Norwegian Church (*c.*1991 Michael Watts). The very moving 'Merchant Seafarers War Memorial' (1994–6 Brian Fell) depicting a ship's hull and a drowned sailor's face is prominently placed near the Senedd. Captain Robert Falcon Scott whose ship '*Terra Nova*' set sail from Cardiff on June 15th, 1910 at the beginning of his ill-fated expedition to reach the South Pole, is commemorated in front of the Norwegian Church by a white mosaic sculpture showing him looking out to sea (2009 Jonathan Williams). Nine Ruabon brick sculptures called 'Beastie Benches' (1994 Gwen Heeney) act as seats near the Lightship. First offices, then cafés, restaurants and shops, apartment blocks, Techniquest and Cardiff Bay Hotel appeared, but the Bay's commercial success was assured when the Millennium Centre opened in 2004, built instead of Zaha Hadid's competition-winning design for an opera house. The architect chosen in a second competition was Jonathan Adams of the firm of Percy Thomas, construction by Sir Robert McAlpine, acoustic by Aarup Acoustics.

Adams' vision of the building reflected Wales in the materials, so Welsh slate and steel is used on the outside and Welsh hardwoods inside. Salvaged slate unsuitable for roofing can be seen in the outer walls; purple slate from Penrhyn, blue from Cwrt y Bugail, green from Nantlle Valley, black from Corris and grey from Llechwedd. The domed roof is covered with Monmouthshire textured steel sections riveted together and coloured with copper oxide, reflecting Wales' industrial history. Of course, the acoustic in the auditorium makes all sound near perfect. The outstanding feature of the exterior has to be words cut into gleaming copper composed by Welsh poet Gwyneth Lewis: '*Creu gwir fel gwydr o ffwrnais awen*' meaning '*Creating truth like glass from the furnace of inspiration*' and intertwined, the line '*In these stones horizons sing*'. Gwyneth Lewis said that she wanted '*the words to reflect the architecture of the building. Its copper dome reminded me of the furnaces from Wales's industrial heritage and also Ceridwen's cauldron, from which the early poet Taliesin received his*

The Millennium Centre, opened in 2000 designed by Jonathan Adams.

inspiration'. She wanted the English words to have their own message and so added another idea saying '... *The stones inside the theatre literally sing with opera, musicals and orchestral music, and I wanted to convey the sense of an international space created by the art of music.*' Inside, native hardwoods create the waving pattern of the galleries and the random spacing of the supporting columns evokes the feeling of a forest made from shining fossilised tree trunks.

Near the Millenium Centre is a sculpture of Ivor Novello (2009 Peter Nicholas), composer of the gorgeous 'When Nightingales sang in Berkeley Square' and the poignant 'Keep the Home Fires Burning' among other songs and musicals and who spent his early years in Cardiff.

Craft in the Bay opposite the Millenium Centre is a showcase and gallery of The Makers Guild in Wales displaying a wide variety of art and craft work including glass, paintings, ceramics, fabrics and fashion. The building itself, originally called D Shed and listed Grade II because of its unusual iron frame was moved from another docklands site.

The **Senedd**, opened by Queen Elizabeth II on St David's Day in 2006, is by Richard Rogers Partnership, construction by Taylor Woodrow. The design concept was one of openness and transparency. Warmth is given by the use of wood, most strikingly by the curving timbers of the porch and inside, the intriguing funnel made of Canadian Red cedar. This defines the *siambr* or debating chamber below, where the desks are bespoke hand-made furniture of Welsh oak. Siambr proceedings can be watched from a gallery. The Senedd is described as

1. Bronze of 'People Like Us' 1993 John Clinch;
2. The Leisure Pool in the International Sports Village.

Wales during the mid 20th century, ruled by the French chef M. Hulot who is commemorated by a plaque beside the main door. Landsea House (1903) next to the dry dock was the office of Mount Stuart Graving Co. The attractive pilotage building now a restaurant is thought to have been built originally as stables for Lord Bute.

Cardiff Bay cannot be left without a brief mention of **Techniquest** and the **International Sports Village**. Techniquest occupies a former industrial building and is Cardiff's science and discovery museum, a paradise for children, with amazing models and devices which they can work. The International Sports Village towards Penarth has a 50m Olympic pool with a Leisure Pool next door full of light and colour; a network of tube slides snake from high above and water seems to be everywhere. The Bay Ice Arena and White Water rafting are also part of this complex.

Bute Street is long and straight, laid down by the 2nd Marquess of Bute. It begins in Cardiff Bay and ends at the **Golden Cross** pub. Behind the mile-long wall is the railway that he insisted should connect the town to the Docks.

Most of the historic buildings of Bute

green and energy-mean with automatic ventilation and minimal air conditioning. The roof-top cowl funnels light and air into the siambr below and expels hot air. Near to the Senedd the former Big Windsor hotel on the Butetown Link Road was one of the most famous restaurants in

Street are at the seaward end and are briefly described below.

The Packet public house whose exterior is little changed since it opened. The 'Mary Ann' backs of Nos. 2-12 Bute Crescent opposite were revealed when Nos. 118-129 Bute Street were demolished and became the **Eli Jenkins** and **Jolyon** pubs – these are not in Bute Street, but should be mentioned.

The colourful former **Midland Bank**, Nos 97–100 Bute Street (1874, extended 1902–3 and 1914–15 by F. Cutlan) in grey and pink granite, Bath stone, terracotta and yellow brick. Carved stone swags (*fruit and flowers on ropes or ribbons*) and ornamental brackets at the top add a final flourish.

E.G. Rivers of the Office of Works designed the splendid **Old Post Office** in Bute Place. It opened in 1881 as the Telegraph & Mercantile Marine departments of the Board of Trade. Its gorgeous colouring makes it an outstanding dockland building, but at the time of writing it has been empty for many years.

Cory's Building (1889 Bruton & Williams) was built by the Cory shipping family when it moved to Cardiff and became one of the most successful shipping enterprises of the time.

Next door is the little **Custom House** (1898 by Henry Tanner), also empty for many years. Tanner was the chief architect to the Office of Works and also designed the Westgate Street section of the former Post Office (1894-7) and another fine Post Office in Newport, Gwent.

Opposite are the elegant fluted pillars of the **National Westminster Bank** (1924-27 F.C.R. Palmer & W.F.C. Holden), now a social venue whose front elevation is in West Bute Street where the door is surmounted by a bronze of "Equity" (J. A. Stevenson). If it is open go in to see the former banking hall.

Continuing north, and to the right, is **Dock Chambers** (*c*.1875), the offices, gallery and education centre of **Butetown History & Arts Centre. BayArt** at No. 54b/c is the gallery and studios of **Butetown Artists**.

Pascoe House, No. 54 (1875 William Blessley) in High Victorian semi-Gothic Venetian style was one of the first showpiece buildings of the docks, intended to impress the business competitors of its owners, Powell Duffryn

Coal Co. William Blessley often used many different stones in his buildings, set like crazy paving to unusual effect.

The group of buildings ends with **Bute Road Railway Station** (*c*.1843) probably designed by Brunel and one of the earliest surviving railway buildings in the country.

It is now some distance up mile-long Bute Street to reach the next group of interesting buildings.

The Priory Church of St Mary at the northern end of Bute Street was the full name of the St Mary's (founded *c*.1100) on the banks of the Taff which gave its name to St Mary Street. After the 1607 great flood (page 26) that church was so badly damaged that it was abandoned and eventually collapsed, leaving the parish without its own church, so the present St Mary's opened in Bute Street to replace it. While the parish raised £5,700, the 2nd Marquess of Bute gave £1,000 and the land. To aid fund-raising, four poets, including the Poet Laureate William Wordsworth, were asked to compose a poem which would be printed and sold. Wordsworth's sonnet.[7]

Bute Road Railway Station built 1842-3 at the 3rd Marquess of Bute's insistence and has been restored as offices. A small station ends the line named Cardiff Bay Station.

'When Severn's sweeping flow had overthrown
St Mary's Church, the Preacher then would cry,
'Thus Christian people, God His might hath shown,
That ye to him your love may testify;
Haste and rebuild the pile.' But not a stone
Resumed its place – age after age went by,
And Heaven still lacked its due, though piety
In secret did, we trust, her loss bemoan.

But now her Spirit hath put forth its claim
In power, and Poesy would lend her voice,
Let the new work be worthy of its aim,
That in its beauty Cardiff may rejoice!
Oh, in the past if cause there was for shame,
Let not our times halt in their better choice!'

Almost at the top Bute Street opens out into **Callaghan Square**, overlooked by the Salvation Army Hostel, and the offices of Eversheds. A bronze of the 2nd Marquess of Bute by John Evan Thomas, which used to be at the southern end of St Mary Street, dignifies this fine piazza which is enclosed by French-style pollarded trees.

The **Golden Cross** pub (c.1903-4) marks the top end of Bute Street. With its colourful tiling and leaded 'Brains' windows, its Grade II listed status allowed it to remain stubbornly amid modern development. Inside are tiled pictures of the original Town Hall, Cardiff Castle and Brains Brewery. It is popular with the gay community.

1. The Priory Church of St Mary's, Bute Street (1845) designed by Bristol architect Thomas Foster in a Norman style reminiscent of the buildings illustrated in medieval manuscripts; 2. Details of the tiles outside the Golden Cross (c.1903-4).

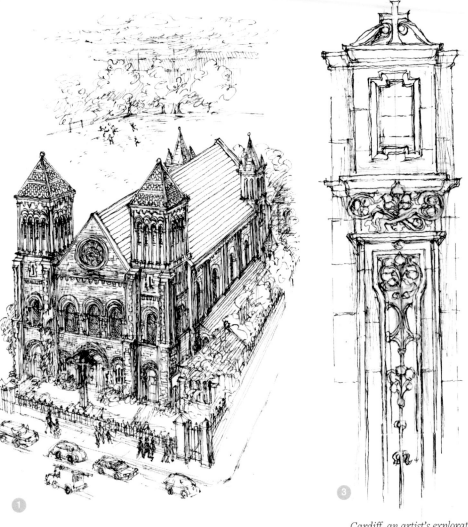

9. Westgate Street to Cathays Park

Principality Stadium, Cardiff Castle, St Mary Street, The Hayes and Queen Street

To reach Cardiff Castle from the Golden Cross along Westgate Street turn left and pass a fine sculpture 'All Hands' (2001 by Brian Fell). The former Custom House (c.1845, 1865 and 1983-5) on East Canal Wharf, along with West Canal Wharf opposite, was on the canal basin of the Glamorganshire Canal. Across the road is the **Great Western Hotel** (1875) designed by W.D. Blessley in his working of the French Gothic and using 'crazy paving' stonework, grand enough to entice travellers arriving at **Central Station**. This impressive building (1932-4) is by the G.W.R. Architects' Department. The Booking Hall is minus its original booking desks, but is a superb space with a high barrel-vaulted ceiling and 1930's light fittings. **Central Square** replaced the bus terminus in front of the station and was completed in 2018.

To get to **Westgate Street** from the Great Western Hotel go into St Mary Street then into Wood Street, marked by **O'Neill's** on the corner of the huge **Royal Hotel** extension (1890, J.P. Jones). The rest of the Royal Hotel is in St Mary Street (1864-66 C.E. Bernard). Beside the Royal Hotel the **Pierhead Clock** (c.1897) in a glass case displays the mechanism; it had been sold to an American after removal from the Pierhead Building but he eventually brought it back and gave it to Cardiff. The three monkeys are a reference to the 3rd Marquess of Bute's antagonism to Darwin's theory of evolution.

Wetherspoons in Wood Street, formerly the **Prince of Wales Theatre** (1878 Blessley & Waring) overlooks the northern end of Westgate Street. A provision of the planning permission for conversion of this Grade II listed building was that it must be possible to return it to use as a theatre if required at some time in the future. The architects ingeniously designed a restaurant in the dress circle retaining the proscenium arch, stage and boxes. Reliefs of classical scenes decorate the proscenium and some boxes bizarrely remain on the walls. A 'pod' was created downstairs for different uses in what had been the stalls.

Past the 1970s offices, the former **Post Office** (Henry Tanner *c.*1894-9) was extended into Park Street in 1907 as County Court Offices. The buildings are crowned with a wonderful arrangement of Classical decorative pediments, pinnacles, sculpture and steep roofs. The **County Club** (*c.*1890 E.M.W. Corbett) and The WRU Store stand isolated in front of the main entrance to the Millennium Stadium. **The WRU Store** was originally Jackson Hall (1878 G.E. Robinson).

Jackson Hall (1878 G.E. Robinson) was built as a covered raquets hall, and is now The WRU Store.

The Millennium Stadium was completed in time to host the 1999 Rugby World Cup, an outstanding year for Cardiff and Wales although Australia became the new world champions. St Mary Street, High Street and the Castle were hung with flags and bunting, the atmosphere electric as the Stadium opened with a friendly when Wales beat South Africa. Success did not continue for Wales as Argentina beat them in the opening match. Many more matches have been played since 1999, sometimes with the splendid sliding roof drawn over the pitch. Most prestigious of all are rugby internationals when it is nigh on impossible to obtain a ticket. Crowds of fans fill the streets, pubs and cafés. Vendors of red, white and green scarves, flags and hats compete with others selling the colours of the opposition.

The construction of the Millennium Stadium resulted in the demolition of Wales Empire Pool, a major loss, and the demolition of part of Cardiff Arms Park. The Stadium was actually designed in 1962 to seat 74,000 people, the largest in Britain at the time and at an estimated cost of £130 million. The final cost was nearer to £170 million. The architects were Hok & Lobb Partnership, W.S. Atkins the engineers and construction by John Laing plc. The pitch was laid on pallets so that the turf could be removed for concerts and rallies of all kinds including events as diverse as motor racing and school netball tournaments. This was not entirely successful and in 2014 a Desso surface which intertwines grass turf with millions of artificial fibres took the place of the original turf.

In 1998, with excitement and sorrow I climbed into the score box and spent hours sketching the demolition and building work that proceeded together. The vast space was dotted with lorries, diggers, cement mixers and scaffolding whilst water cascaded dramatically down the old South Stand. Reinforced concrete foundations and basement spaces were being laid simultaneously with demolition of the Arms Park, so there were criss-cross patterns of steel rods in the foreground. Lilliputian workmen populated the site and Fitzalan Embankment was a toy town in the background. When it was time to demolish the score box I was no longer allowed on the site, even with a helmet, and had to be content with sketching outside. In the winter it was freezing, but I could not resist trying to capture the strangeness of the huge enclosure, the delicate scaffolding draped with safety nets and triffidesque cranes crouching over apparent chaos. It was truly exciting and challenging to study the structure of masts and cables and see the tiny figures of men working at the tops of masts, or on the huge triangular structures jutting from the corners like ships' prows thrusting out, or part of some space ship, a reminder of the film *Star Wars*. One wintry day I recorded the dismantling of a giant crane alongside Wood Street, reputed to be the largest in Britain, which had been used to manoeuvre the then revolutionary sliding roof into position and install a corner mast.

The **Millennium Stadium** shot Cardiff into the 21st century. Utterly contemporary

1 & 2. *Building the Millennium Stadium;*
3. *Demolishing Cardiff Arms Park whilst building the Millennium Stadium.*

in concept, it seemed ready to take off into space, ready to float into the upper atmosphere among the planets. In 2016 it was renamed to acknowledge its new sponsor: Principality Stadium.

Don't miss the 1930s relief of Queen's and Royal Garage over the windows of **Zerodegrees Restaurant** opposite the Stadium. **Queen's Vault**, another tiled pub, is on the corner of Golate, so-called, it is said, because people would hurry down that lane to the town quay on the Taff, fearing they would be late: the real version is that that name is a derivation of 'Golly's Lane'. Further along Westgate Street one passes converted warehouses and Wetherspoon's **The Gate Keeper**, originally a theatre. A tall narrow brick building that was the Cardiff Ladies Club ends this row of buildings. **Castle Court Flats** opposite date from the 1930s. Finally, the side elevation of the **Angel Hotel** (*c.*1890 William Frame) Cardiff's most historic hotel where visiting rugby teams stay, and which has a splendid entrance hall with a sweeping staircase. During the 18th and 19th centuries the old **Angel Hotel** and the **Cardiff Arms Hotel** nearby, owned by the 1st Marquess of Bute, were two of the most important coaching inns

William Burges 1827-1881.

in town. The Cardiff Arms had a lawn with a weeping ash tree in whose shade people would dine. The entrance to the **Cardiff Rugby Club** ground is on the junction with Castle Street.

Turn right from Westgate Street into Castle Street,

and the entrance to Cardiff Castle. On the corner of Womanby Street **Elevens Bar & Grill** and **Clwb Ifor Bach** (see p. 14) is on the site of another 18th century pub. Alternatively cross the road to see the **Animal Wall**. There are two groups of animals: those with shining glass eyes were designed by Burges, carved by William Nicholls and are muscular lions bearing the Bute coat of arms, a lioness, a sea lion, a lynx and monkeys. Lord Bute was very keen to have the animals painted in natural colours, and this was done although Nicholls disagreed with him. Was Nicholls right, or would coloured animals continue the medieval decorative scheme of the Clock Tower? The 4th Marquess added six more animals carved in more angular style by Edinburgh sculptor A.

The 3rd Marquess of Bute 1847-1900.

Carrick in 1930. Enter Bute Park by the West Gate and visit **Pettigrew's**, a charming café in the little building that was formerly Bute West Lodge (1860-62

Alexander Roos). William Pettigrew was Cardiff Corporation's Head Gardener. West Lodge had been unused for many years and was taken on as a project by Cardiff Building Preservation Trust and Cardiff Council who restored it as a dwelling. After some years it was taken over and converted into the café with Burges designed floor tiles lifted for safe keeping by Victorian Society members from the Blackfriars site in Bute Park. Anything by Burges is a collectors' item and the tiles were disappearing over the years.

Cardiff Castle is the glorious heart of Cardiff. Within those massive walls the Victorian interiors glow like jewels. They were designed by William Burges (1827-81) who, in his own realisation of the Gothic style, transformed the castle into the fantasy we see today.

The 3rd Marquess of Bute was Burges' patron and close friend at Oxford University where the young Lord Bute was a student at Christ Church College. Both shared a passion for Gothicism and mysticism, underlined for Lord Bute by his leaning towards the Roman Catholic faith. He strayed from his strict Presbyterian upbringing to the dismay of his family, converting when he came of age. Still a student aged only eighteen, he was so impressed by Burges that he commissioned him to carry out an architectural report on the castle.

William or 'Billy' Burges, as his friends called him, was born in London and educated at King's College School where his near contemporaries included brothers Dante Gabriel and William Michael Rossetti and where their drawing master was probably John Sell Cotman. He did a year's training in engineering and then took up architectural articles, falling under the spell of Augustus Welby Pugin, the leading Gothicist of the day. Burges had private means enabling him to travel widely in pursuit of his passion for the Gothic, gaining an international reputation as a medievalist, filling sketchbooks with notes and drawings from which he was able to build up designs. He was particularly enthralled by Chillon, a lake-side castle in Switzerland and used many of its features in his buildings. Although he had entered and won architectural competitions, his career really began, aged thirty-five, with a commission for St Finbar's Cathedral in Cork, Republic of Ireland. Short, chubby, very short-sighted and with a pug nose, his energy was extraordinary. He died aged only fifty-three, seemingly from overwork, having achieved an incredible amount in his short career.

When he came of age in 1868 and with £300,000, Lord Bute immediately engaged Burges to restore Cardiff Castle. 'Restore' might be the wrong word since, although Burges's designs were Gothic in origin, he made the style uniquely his own. Together Lord Bute and Burges worked on the castle for the next sixteen years (1865-81), Bute involving himself with the choice of subject and symbolism of each room. In 1869 work began on the fabulous Clock

Tower using the original Roman foundations, which took four years to complete. The use of colour on the exterior stems from the Gothic practice of colouring architecture, surprising to us, accustomed as we are to romantic images of ruined grey abbeys and churches and to seeing natural stone in historic buildings. The symbolism of the Clock Tower begins outside with starry skies and figures representing the seven planets with signs of the zodiac on their pedestals. Within the Clock Tower the glittering bachelor apartments (begun before Lord Bute's marriage) rise one above the other, culminating in the most magnificent interior of all – the Summer Smoking Room. Brightly coloured one-third lifesized figures representing the eight winds of classical antiquity gaze out from the four corners. Mosaics make a circular pattern on the floor and a gold chandelier supporting a golden Apollo hangs from the midnight blue ceiling which is set with shining stars made from concave glass. A truly wonderful creation.

Lady Gwendolen Howard, a society beauty, married Lord Bute in 1872. Perhaps

to be on the safe side as he welcomed his bride, he chose conventional silk hangings for her apartments, but she was soon drawn into the restoration going on around her, taking a special interest in the

Cardiff Castle Clock Tower from Duke Street.

The Lodgings at Cardiff Castle. The complete range of buildings from the west is shown on page 14.

Chaucer Room, her own sitting room. It is also one of my favourites because of its murals of trees and representations of graceful birds. '*The Legend of Good Women*' who were eight love-stricken ladies from antiquity, and characters from '*The Canterbury Tales*' are depicted in the stained glass windows of the lantern. Each visitor will have their favourite room, but who cannot but be awed by the Banqueting Hall, charmed by the Nursery,

want to read in the Library or wish that they could spend a night in Lord Bute's Gothic bedroom. The Arab Room was his favourite. Its exotic muquarnas ceiling (*an Arabian system of vaulting*) is made of wood, covered with stencilled patterns and gold leaf; parrots are another feature. The Arab Room, commissioned shortly before Burges' death, has the words '*John, Marquess of Bute built this in 1881, William Burges designed it*' carved onto the white marble mantelpiece in Burges' distinctive use of Lombardic uncials (*a style of 16th century lettering*). The Butes' love of antiquity is also reflected in the Roof Garden following a visit they made to Pompeii. An added bonus is that one passes by Burges' delicate Gothic flèche on the Beauchamp Tower carved from wood and finished with lead.

Ornamental chimney pieces carved of stone with historical or mythological scenes in keeping with their themes dominate the main rooms. Many rooms have some richly coloured stained glass, marquetry (*inlaid designs of different materials, but mostly wood*) shutters and carved and painted animals or birds, climbing round doorways or hiding in some nook. There was no end to Burges' inventiveness as hundreds of beautifully drawn and coloured designs poured from his studios. The **Cardiff Castle Collections** contain over two thousand drawings, designs and stained glass cartoons. Of course, none of this would have happened without the group of artists and craftsmen Burges gathered to work on the castle, based in workshops at the castle, in Tyndall Street and in North Road. Among them were: his chief architectural assistant William Frame; John Starling Chapple, architect and office manager; Horatio Walter Lonsdale, artist; sculptors Thomas Nicholls, William Clarke of Llandaff, Thomas John and his son William Goscombe John; Fred Weekes, designer, especially of glass, and the decorating firm of Campbell Smith & Co. These are perhaps the most well-known, but there was a host of tile and glass makers, stonemasons, wood carvers, joiners and marquetry artists. I would love to have been one of the artists.

It all cost money, a lot of money, but then the 3rd Marquess of Bute was one of the richest men in the world.

After Burges' premature death in 1881 the grieving Butes and their team of artists and craftsmen continued the work under the direction of William Frame. Following World War II the castle was given to the people of Cardiff by the 5th Marquess. At that time Victorian architecture – and Cardiff Castle – had fallen seriously out of fashion. The Victorian Society, founded in

Cardiff Castle in the late 19th century showing the animal wall and some vines.

1968 by a group of artists, architects, architectural historians and other concerned people angered by demolitions of fine 19th century buildings, drew attention to the threat to the nation's Victorian heritage and its value to our towns and cities. One casualty of anti-Victorianism was that the Burges decorations and fittings partly completed at Knightshayes (in Somerset) were removed or painted over by the owners, a fate that fortunately did not befall Cardiff Castle when, in 1949, it was turned into the Welsh College of Music and Drama. In 1974 the College moved to new buildings and Cardiff Corporation began to refurbish the castle, buying Burges furniture and fittings – at vastly inflated prices – and making the Castle more accessible. As Victorian architecture gained popularity the 3rd Marquess of Bute and William Burges' Gothic fantasy came to be more universally appreciated and its beauty marvelled at once again.

High Street, leading into **St Mary Street** opposite the main entrance to Cardiff Castle has been the town centre since medieval times. Here were the Church of St Mary the Virgin, the Guildhall and the town jail or 'cwchmoel.'

Cardiff Castle Clock Tower from the Bailey.

Since pedestrianisation High Street and St Mary Street have been changed from being noisy, crowded, unfriendly streets into pleasant open spaces with little traffic. Some buildings are very tall and narrow, most in a 19th century version of gothic, classical or baroque styles in brick, stone or stucco (*plaster*). Sadly, many upper floors have been empty for years, some valuable buildings closed and with little prospect of change for the better during the early 21st century although by 2019 there was a general feeling that these empty spaces could be made into accommodation to help resolve the housing crisis and revive the town centre.

High Street begins with the **Goat Major** pub which honours the Royal 41st Regiment North Wales of the Royal Welsh Fusiliers' mascot. One goat was given to them by Queen Victoria from her flock of Kashmir goats, but the Fusiliers have had a goat mascot since the 18th century. The present magnificent long-haired goat is named Llewelyn. The Regiment also has a sketch of "Taffy" a previous one by Kyffin Williams. The classical style shop opposite (1835) was built as the National Provincial Bank but the shop front is a modern reproduction. Next to this, two buildings in a Victorian mix of styles and then the entrance to **High Street Arcade** (1885 T. Waring & Son, J.P. Jones) a colourful version of Gothic and Renaissance styles leading to Trinity Street. **Duke Street**

Arcade (1902 Ware & Williams) branches from it to Duke Street.

Castle Arcade (1887 Peter Price) goes from High Street to Castle Street; it has wooden first floor walkways and balustrades linked by foot bridges that reflect Cardiff's maritime history. Another feature is the large mirrors on the upstairs end walls enhancing the light and space. The High Street end of the arcade is completely different to the Castle Street end, in yellow brick and prettily decorated with 'Wedgewood' green. Almost next door, **No. 20** High Street has a delightful stone relief of animals over the window. Church Street and Quay Street mark the beginning of **St Mary Street**. The corner shop dates from the mid-19th century.

The cavernous entrance to the **Central Market** (1886) was designed by J.P. Jones (1886) and is on the site of 'the Drop', a gruesomely descriptive name for the public gallows. In 1883 Alderman John Winstone wrote of '*the street entrance to the place of execution in St Mary Street. It had a very ugly appearance from its bare neglected walls, cross beam and platform.*' The legendary Dic Penderyn (whose real name was Richard Lewis) was hanged there because he was convicted of stabbing to

The cello room of the Violin Shop, Castle Arcade drawn in 2014.

death one of the soldiers sent by the 2nd Marquess of Bute to quell the 1831 Merthyr Riot of iron workers and coal miners. Penderyn was arrested, taken down to Cardiff jail and, with two other men, was found guilty of fomenting rebellion and condemned to death. Penderyn was the only one of the three to die even though some prominent figures had established his innocence. It seems that a scapegoat was needed to pay for the death of the soldier, sixteen others and the many injuries caused, to act as a warning to potential trouble makers. Penderyn was hanged on August 13th, 1831. His last words were '*O Arglwydd, dyma gamwedd*' '*O Lord, here is an iniquity*'.

When an adjoining building to the 'Drop' and a derelict police station burnt down, both were demolished and the Market built on the site. **Central Market** (1886-91) is by the energetic borough engineer William Harpur who was heavily involved in the public works of late Victorian Cardiff, including Roath Park and Cathays Park. Among his other projects were the **Old Pumping Station** now an antiques market (Penarth Road), Guildford Crescent Baths (demolished), the charming wooden park keepers' lodges in the city parks – as in Gorsedd Gardens – and the isolation hospital on Flat Holm Island. The Central Market has changed little, the stalls grouped round an elevated office to give a good view of everything. Sparrows flutter in the iron roof trusses, and there are more stalls up on the balcony. Definitely the best place in town to get fresh provisions as well as other essentials like kitchen utensils, second hand books, electrical bits and pieces and goldfish.

A passage leads from the Market to Church Street past the Old Arcade pub to the **Owain Glyndŵr,** built on the site of the Mably Arms, dating from 1721. There are large impersonal buildings. Back in St Mary Street **No. 117,** formerly the National Westminster Bank, is grandly ornamented with five different bearded heads over each of the arched windows and decorative mouldings at the first floor windows. **No. 110** has delicate reliefs over its windows of floral wreaths illustrating farming, coal mining, iron making and shipping, the top floor crowned with a bardic harpist. Half caryatids (*sculptures of figures supporting horizontal structures*) support the pediment.

Tall and narrow, the five storey **Borough Arms** is squeezed in beside **Howells** store. The first northern part is by Blessley (1895-6) with delicate Renaissance style reliefs on the pilasters between the windows and fanciful shell niches upstairs. Inside, a first floor department keeps cast iron pillars from Wharton Street Chapel, demolished to build the store. The southern part, added 1928-30, is an example of American Beaux Arts classicism designed by Sir Percy Thomas. The upper corner is ornamented with a stylish relief depicting trade, perhaps the Silk Road; strongly carved angular figures carry various items and a donkey bears a panier of boxes. In 2018 closure of Howells was announced, which together with the closure of David Morgans and Marments seems to mark the end of an era. Another tall narrow pub, **The Cottage** has richly carved ornamentation round the ground floor and first floor bays, and has been there unchanged as long as anyone can remember. A recent addition to St Mary Street is the **Brewery Quarter**, a lively courtyard of bars, restaurants and clubs leading to Caroline Street. **Kitty Flynn's**, a refurbishment of the Cambrian pub, is on the corner. **Wyndham Arcade** (1886) by Peter Price slants its way to The Hayes.

Sadness overtook me in 2014 when researching the southern end of St Mary Street for this book. It was a forlorn sight with the exception of some buildings including the former Costa Rica Coffee

Southern end of St Mary Street in 1987 showing the old Western Mail offices and Barry's Commercial Hotel (1888) now Travelodge.

(1886) was closed. In 2019 the street is coming back to life – The Philharmonic and The Square and No. 75 have been cleaned and repaired, complementing the hotels, bars and restaurants already in business.

Le Monde restaurant occupies the former Costa Rica Coffee Co., another tall narrow building in brick and stone, richly decorated with heavy swags on each floor. It was one of the biggest importers of coffee in Britain, founded by a Cardiff sea captain and his brother in 1924. Coffee originally came from the Yemen and spread across Europe from its ports, reaching peak demand in the 18th century but the Yemen monopoly was gone when seedlings were smuggled out of the country to Africa, South America and the Dutch East Indies. Coffee drinking in Wales spread from the docks and was especially popular among Italian cafés during the 20th century. The Costa Rica

Co., and **The Peppermint** pub. Hebe was still keeping watch over the entrance to the **Prince of Wales Theatre** (1921), but the shabby **Philharmonic Hall** or **The Square** (1876) built as a music hall was closed. **The Philharmonic,** a once popular pub, was closed and desolate but kept its elegant window frames. Sandwiched between this and Maddison's, **No. 75**, a tall, narrow polychromatic building with Gothic windows and spikey gargoyles

1. Wyndham Arcade (1886) Peter Price, who was instrumental in founding the Free Library (page 90). Drawn from The Hayes to illustrate its extraordinary angle sandwiched between warehouses originally alongside the Glamorganshire Canal;
2. Tabernacle (1865 John Hartland).

Coffee Co. 1940s stock book lists their clients including: Forté in Barry, Severini in Blackwood, Sidoli in Merthyr, Carpanneri in Porth as well as Cardiff cafés and restaurants.[8]

From the **Peppermint** pub formerly The Terminus, you can see East and West Canal Wharfves of the Glamorganshire Canal basin and canal. A short detour under the bridge takes you to **Jacob's Antiques Market and Gallery** in a former warehouse open Wednesday to Saturday 10.00am-4.00pm. Otherwise turn sharp left from the Peppermint into **Mill Lane** where former Canal side warehouses have been transformed into a lively café quarter.

The **Central Library** (2009 DBP Architects) when it opened it had 90,000 books, of which 10,000 were in Welsh. Another feature is green technology which includes a sedum grass roof, coloured glass panels, solar shading and a full Building Management System providing climatic control to all three floors. A large abstract sculpture – 'Alliance' (2009 Jean-Bernard Métais) dominates Hayes Place outside. Beside the Library are **John Lewis** and **St David's 2** (2009 by Benoy with Building Design Partnership) and the apartments in **The Hayes** by Glen

Royal Arcade (1858 Peter Price) going to St Mary Street is the earliest arcade. **Morgan Arcade** (1896 Edwin Seward) is beside the **David Morgan** building. This was one of Cardiff's well-loved independent family stores designed by a group of architects that included Edwin Seward who designed the central section in 1899, with later additions in 1904 and 1912 by James & Morgan, and is now apartments above the shops below. The original panelled tea room with decorations of painted flowers has been retained as a lounge within the complex.

A statue of industrialist and Liberal M.P. John Batchelor, 'The Friend of Freedom' (1885 James Milo ap Griffith) gestures grandly along The Hayes. The opposition party petitioned the Town Council to remove it, and feeling was so strong that in 1887 he was daubed with coal tar and paint. Behind him, Hayes Island Snack Bar in front of the Old Library is shaded by wonderful mature plane trees. There cannot be many open air cafés where you sit beside the ornamental railings of two listed 19th century underground public conveniences. The snack bar itself was originally the tram parcels depot and greatly expanded by 2018.

Howells. In complete contrast to the 19th century shops and arcades of The Hayes, **Grand Arcade**, the centre-piece of St David's 2 passes like a shining nave through this cathedral of consumerism to link with **St David's 1** and **Queen Street**.

Northwards along The Hayes the 'Duke of Wellington' is next to **Capel Tabernacl** (*c.*1865), a fine classical building designed by John Hartland to replace an earlier chapel. There is an old cholera graveyard behind it. Beside Tabernacle,

The Old Library
(1896 James, Seward & Thomas).

The Central Library, as the **Old Library** was called before its closure, was opened in 1896. Its story goes back to the 1850-55 Free Libraries Act when local architect Peter Price, who was making strenuous efforts to establish a Cardiff library, set up a voluntary library in a room above the entrance to the Royal Arcade which he had designed. Cardiff was the first Welsh local authority to provide a free public library, but it took another twenty-one years for the first part of the Central Library to be completed. In the meantime a library and newly founded museum was established in the Y.M.C.A. then at 79 St Mary Street.

James, Seward & Thomas won the architectural competition for the new library (there were 128 entries) with Edwin Seward's design. Copies of local newspapers, the London *Times* and a specimen of each coin of the realm were placed within the hollowed-out foundation stone laid by the Mayor in 1880. The library was built in two parts, the first part being the northern one-third nearest St John's; it also contained the Museum and Schools of Art & Sciences and was completed in 1882. The southern part, crowned by a bust of Pallas Athene (Minerva to some), was opened in 1896 by Edward, Prince of Wales. The imposing main doorway is surmounted by classical beauties representing Study and Rhetoric. After a period of uncertainty, the Old Library has become the hub of **Menter Iaith Caerdydd** – the Welsh language promoter in the capital. It also houses the Cardiff Museum or **The Cardiff Story** as it is called, a gallery and offices upstairs. Tiles by artist and illustrator Walter Crane can be seen in the entrance to the bar in the 1882 section. The **Wales Tourist Information Centre** is on the ground floor also entered from Working Street.

St David's Hall, no longer the newest concert hall and theatre in Cardiff, was opened in 1982. The architects, Seymour Harris Partnership, faced a very challenging task as the building was to seat 2000 spectators, have state of the art acoustics (up-dated in 2004) and had to be fitted onto a cramped, awkwardly shaped site. They built into and on top of the partly built St David's Centre, also by J. Seymour Harris Partnership built 1979-82, hence St David's Hall's unusual shape. The angular concrete shapes of the exterior make it something of a period piece but its interior is still the venue for prestigious events and exhibitions. The golden Stuttgart stained glass window (1984-5) dominates Level 3. Near St David's Hall the overpowering entrance to **Queen's Arcade** (1992-3 Taylor Group) connects to St David's Centre.

Nearly all the exterior of **St John's** except the tower dates from the 19th century and is best appreciated from Working Street and the graveyard garden. (For St John's early history see page 12) The 19th century work was begun by John Prichard who was working on the restoration of Llandaff Cathedral at the time, and continued after his death by architects Kempson & Fowler. They

St John's Church drawn from Working Street. Founded c.1180.

Sir William Goscombe John and the east window above was designed by Sir Ninian Comper. A 'Father' Henry Willis organ was installed in 1894. Work on the interior continued in the 19th and 20th centuries with Morris & Co. windows and another designed by Prichard's assistant J.P. Seddon illustrating *'Suffer the little children to come unto me'* in light browns, pinks, mauves and indigos. Welsh soldiers of the Burma Campaign who lost their lives during the construction of the notorious Burma Railway are commemorated in another window donated by the Burma Star Association in 1986.

Sir Ninian Comper's reredos in the Chapel of the Order of St John, completed in 1916, is composed of delicately beautiful gilded enamels illustrating the Annunciation, the Nativity, saints and angels.

Before **Queen Street** was named in honour of Queen Victoria in 1886 it was called Crokertown (or Crokherbtown). The name survives in Crokerherbtown Lane parallel to Queen Street which was part of the main route from England into Wales until pedestrianisation when traffic was re-routed along the specially constructed Boulevard de Nantes, named

removed the galleries, which had been installed to accommodate large congregations during the 18th century, replacing the south and north walls by two aisles and enlarging and raising the nave in Prichard's favourite pointed style. Prichard also designed the intricate stone reredos (*a screen behind and above the altar*) carved by a master mason at Clarke's of Llandaff, but the gilded figures of Old Testament prophets are by Welsh sculptor

after one of Cardiff's twin towns. Queen Street is thought by some have less architectural value than St Mary Street, but it does have an interesting mixture of buildings ranging from 19th century Venetian to the 1993s.

Buildings I find unusual and interesting are briefly described below:

Queen Street Chambers (1878) by E.C. Bernard which contained Queen Street Arcade. It was restored and converted into shops in 1983.

A bronze statue of **Aneurin Bevan** (1987 Robert Thomas) founder of the National Health Service marks the beginning of Queen Street. **Santander Bank** (*c.*1930s) is

amusingly ornamented with a pair of elephant heads. Nearby, **Starbucks** (1930s) has red and blue Egyptian style ornamentation perhaps by the same architect. The most striking building must be **Queen Street Chambers** (c.1878 C.E. Bernard), restored and painted yellow and white in 1983. The colourful building seems incongruous now, but Bernard must

Nos. 9-11 Park Place (1875-6) by William Blessley were the subject of an eleventh hour spot-listing by Cadw in 1986.

have been inspired by the Glamorganshire Canal which passed nearby. Architects were also influenced by John Ruskin's book 'The Stones of Venice' and his exquisite watercolours of its buildings.

Opposite, giant pillars and windows are a reminder of the grand interior of the former **Marments** store (1922-3) dominated by a sweeping staircase to hats and ladies' fashions. **Lloyds TSB** has a bizarre upper elevation decorated with bearded strong men and delicate maiden caryatids. **Queen's Arcade** (1992-3 Taylor Group) connects to **St David's Centre 1** (1979-82 J. Seymour Harris Partnership). A striking Welsh dragon rampant mosaic enlivens the 1950s **Boots** elevation. The **Midland Bank** (1919 Woodfall & Eccles) is the only listed building in Queen Street, so there was some opposition when the Ionic pillars and windows were lengthened in the late 20th century to lighten the interior. **Andrews Buildings** opposite has its date, 1896, encircled by carvings over the doorway and curving plant reliefs between the simple bay windows. During refurbishment in 2009, **Marks & Spencer** was given a glass extension to its café where you can contentedly sip your coffee and enjoy a scone whilst looking through the tree tops to the shoppers below. **W.H. Smith** (1885) is busily decorated with sculpted foliage and heads, all painted white. Is it by the same fanciful architect as Lloyds TSB back down the street?

The giant **Parc Hotel** (1884 Habershon & Fawckner) cost £40,000 to build. It originally had two public halls, one of which became a cinema, ten shops and a coffee house. Round the corner in **Park Place Nos. 9-11** (1875 William Blessley) were the subject of an eleventh hour spot-listing in 1986 when the neglected buildings were about to be demolished. The Victorian Society had strongly opposed the proposed redevelopment for many years and members were delighted when they were listed and refurbished. In 2019 a plan for a large block of student flats on the corner wih Stuttgarter Strasse is being considered. Opposite, the former **South Wales Institute of Engineers** (1893 E.W. Corbett) is decorated with terra cotta reliefs and is now part of clubland. **The New Theatre** (1905-6 Runz & Ford) is the only survivor of many active theatres in early 20th century Cardiff. Until 2000 it was the home of the Welsh National Opera now based in the Millennium Centre.

Park Place continues north to the Civic Centre (page 103).

Charles Street was home to prosperous middle class families during the mid to late 19th century. It had a private school, three places of worship and the vicarage of St John's, now the Friends Meeting House. Charles Street has been through periods of decay, a threat of demolition and has lost some of it terraced houses to modern development but still has much of its 19th century character.

St David's Cathedral (1884-7) was designed by Peter Paul, son of leading Gothicist Augustus Welby Pugin. Peter Paul practised with Pugin & Pugin of Newport. St David's was damaged in the 1939-45 war and restored by diocesan architect F.R. Bates, Son & Price in the 1950s. The fine stained glass of *c.*1910 survived war-time damage, but to my 21st century eyes the 1950s diamond patterned reredos is a strange feature of the restoration.

Capel Ebeneser (1854-5) has a chequered history. It was designed by R.G. Thomas of Newport as Charles Street Congregational Church made, it is said, of stones brought to the docks as ballast in returning coal ships. You might have guessed that he must have been influenced by 'crazy paving' William Blessley who did the schoolroom downstairs. When the original Capel Ebeneser was demolished to make way for St David's Centre, the members

Capel Ebeneser (1854-5).

moved to Charles Street and the Congregationalists moved to City Church, Windsor Place. After a period spent as a facility for St David's Cathedral, Ebeneser became a restaurant.

Turn left into Bridge Street and then left into Churchill Way beside **The Chapel**

Restaurant and Bar which was a refurbishment in 2012-13 of Capel Pembroke Terrace (1887) designed by Henry Harris. However, a tall, ugly development spoils its setting. This majestic French-Gothic chapel with its pointed windows, turrets and semi-cylindrical stair towers was not in the English style favoured at the time. The journal *The Builder* sarcastically opined that *'at this rate of progress in ecclesiastical architecture, the Welsh Calvinists will hardly know themselves soon'*.

Churchill Way was renamed in the 1960s after the feeder canal along the centre had been filled in. The semi-detached villas dating from the *c.*1860s remain but since the 1960s the eastern side has been redeveloped from the original canal – side residences and warehouses. The sculpture 'A Family Group' (2009 Robert Thomas) marks the junction with Queen Street.

As in other towns, Cardiff's middle class and business areas could suddenly give way to areas of mean, crowded streets. One such in Cardiff was Newtown, home to impoverished immigrants, which included the Edward Street area originally behind Churchill Way and extended south and west towards Mary Ann Street. In his *'Pocket Guide of Cardiff'* John Davies describes how in 1849-50 T.W. Rammell, a Board of Health Inspector, investigated the borough's sanitary conditions. His investigation coincided with an epidemic of cholera and diarrhoea killing 383 people and included observations like *'I inspected No17 Stanley Street ... I counted the persons living in the house; there were 54 persons, men, women and children; they live, eat and sleep all in one room. The smell arising from the room was most over-powering'* and goes on to describe the well (where the Capitol Centre is) used for drinking water: *'I have seen worms in it; the people clamber over the wall for this water, it is like a struggle for life and death'*. There were other equally squalid areas in Cardiff as there were in so many other towns. Another such area was **Jones Court**, Womanby Street, off Castle Street, now charming office units. The achievements of the Victorian era came at a price, but I must not get side-tracked here!

Continue along Churchill Way, back to Queen Street and the Capitol Centre. **The Capitol Centre** (1980s, T.P. Bennett) replaces a group of unlisted but valuable historic buildings. The **Capitol Cinema**

(1920) was of reinforced concrete construction, the interior having a grand staircase, a bar and cafe looking out onto Queen Street, stained glass, glass topped tables and basket chairs. Next to it, the Connaught Rooms, happy meeting place for many couples, and the Edwardian Postagraph. All were demolished in the 1980s together with **Cardiff Y.M.C.A.** (19th century James, Jones & Budgen) and **Cory Memorial Hall** (1896). When the

Y.M.C.A. moved to new premises, the building was used by the Caricature Puppet Theatre until that folded through lack of funding. The Victorian Society and Cardiff Civic Society (then Cardiff 2000) campagned hard to save these unlisted buildings, but to no avail. Over the years the Capitol Cinema and some other properties had become empty and decaying, encouraging developers and planners to consider redevelopment.

1. Cardiff Y.M.C.A. and Cory Hall;
2. The Capitol Cinema (1920).

On a happier note, leafy **Windsor Place** and **St Andrew's Crescent**, as conservation areas, have largely avoided inappropriate changes to the buildings. Windsor Place was built *c.*1850s, it seems by Alexander Roos the Bute Estate architect, and is dominated by **City United Reformed Church** (1865-6 F.T. Pilkington & Bruce Vaughan) for a Scottish congregation drawn down to Cardiff to work in the docks and designed by Edinburgh architect F.T. Pilkington. In 1893 it was remodelled by Bruce E. Vaughan who moved the entrance to the south side and put in the fine jutted hammer-beam roof and angel corbels (*a block supporting a beam or other structure*) after a serious fire in 1910. In 1993-4 the west end was separated from the main body of the church by a glass screen to create chapels in the west end and gallery. The café was added in 1980-81 by Wyn Thomas Partnership. Across Stuttgarter Strasse (Stuttgart is another twin town) St Andrew's Crescent, laid down in the 1850s, encircles **Eglwys Dewi Sant** (1863 Prichard & Seddon with Alexander Roos).

Eglwys Dewi Sant (1863) was begun by Prichard and Seddon (page 156) whose original design of a cruciform plan with a spire had to be reduced because of cost. Some of their building survives, but Alexander Roos finished the church, originally named St Andrew's but taken over and rededicated in 1956 after Dewi Sant in Newport Road was demolished. This had been bombed in World War II and never really recovered.

St Andrews Crescent is one place from which to proceed to Cathays Park.

1. *The Chapel Restaurant (1887) Churchill Way, a splendid French Gothic style building;*
2. *Eglwys Dewi Sant (1863).*

10. Cathays Park

City Hall and Law Courts, National Museum of Wales, Cardiff University, Alexandra Gardens, Bute Park

Cathays Park is known as one of the most splendid and monumental civic Centres in Europe. It includes an astonishing range of early 20th century Edwardian buildings like palaces set round Alexandra Gardens. Buildings of later dates have been added: some are fitting additions but others are not so well suited to this setting.

The name 'Cathays' comes from a partly wooded tract of common land outside the borough recorded in 1682 as 'Cate Hayes' which had been owned by the Herberts of Greyfriars until the 1790s. By 1815 this land had been bought by the Butes who enclosed it and used it as a private park.

Wishing to acquire the land for public open space, Cardiff Corporation made spasmodic approaches to buy some of it, without success. There was also a need to replace the existing Town Hall in St Mary Street (1845) which was too small. The idea of using the Park for civic buildings was first mooted in 1890 when Lord Bute offered to sell 38 acres for £120,000. Lascelles Carr, Editor of the *Western Mail*, was against going '*cap in hand to the Marquess*' thinking the price was '*extortionate*' and '*ridiculous*'. Eventually a group of determined Councillors wrote to

Cardiff City Hall, opened in 1906 by the 4th Marquess of Bute and the Lord Mayor.

As soon as the provisional purchase agreement was signed (1897) the Corporation announced a competition for the design of a Town Hall (Cardiff became a city in 1905) and Law Courts. Lord Bute laid down various conditions including the retention of trees and the line of the existing main roadway, later named King Edward VII Avenue. Crucially, the height of the buildings must be low throughout. The competition assessor was famous architect Alfred Waterhouse, winner of the Manchester Town Hall competition. Manchester Town Hall (built 1868-77) is High Victorian fantasy crowned with a huge tower and spire, which Waterhouse followed with his design for the wonderful Natural History Museum in South Kensington, London (1897). He examined the fifty-six competition entries and selected nine finalists although some had to be discarded because their estimates were unrealistically low. From these Waterhouse made a visionary choice and declared the virtually unknown London firm of Lanchester, Stewart & Rickards' design the winner. Baroque was the up and coming architectural fashion: in Cardiff the Pierhead Building and Cathedral Road High Victorian was still the in thing.

Lord Bute suggesting public uses for the land including a new Town Hall, Assize Court, Technical Schools and a University College. The Marquess liked this idea and the Corporation bought the whole 60 acre park for £161,000 in 1898.

The Law Courts showing the original Magistrates' entrance. When they moved to Fitzalan Road in 1990 (p. 127) this became part of the Crown Court.

The Lanchester, Stewart & Rickards practice had been put together specifically to enter architectural competitions. Henry Vaughan Lanchester, brother of the celebrated auto-engineer, was an engineer too, but also an architectural planner.

less well known: he retired from the practice in 1901 and died shortly afterwards.

Edwin Rickards was largely self-taught. He began working life in his mother's Fulham Road, London, drapery shop but soon moved on to study at the Royal Academy Schools. Feeling that he was making little progress there, he left to study independently at the South Kensington Museum (now the Victoria & Albert Museum) until he was accepted by an architectural practice. At the same time he continued with his drawing studies and became a fine draughtsman, vigorously drawing and re-drawing his ideas in pen and ink.

Rickards's creative use of the Baroque (like Burges with his use of the Gothic) inspired his designs for the Town Hall and Law Courts. He met the difficult design challenge of long and low by conceiving them as visually one building, linked by a strongly moulded cornice (*moulding round the top of a wall*), the windows and corner pavilions. He gave drama to his composition with the dome, towers and sculpture.

The builders were the firm of E. Turner & Sons which had begun as a small business operating from Fitzalan

Lanchester's brilliance as a planner enabled the practice to realise Rickards' designs for both buildings. He based them on a classicism developed from special studies in Austria, southern Germany and the Paris Opera. Stewart's contribution is

Embankment and developed into one of the largest construction companies in Wales and the West of England. E. Turner & Sons also built the University, the Coal Exchange, the Old Library and David Morgan's department store. A portrait of James, one of the Turner sons, by Margaret Lyndsey Williams hangs in the City Hall collection. Work was well under way by 1900. A year later the site had eight electrical derrick cranes with eighty steel lattice jibs capable of lifting stones weighing up to five tons, steam cranes and hoists, a stone working plate with a diamond saw, five horizontal frame saws and eleven steam moulding engines. It was also the first building site to have lighting, enabling work to continue after dark. What a noise and how spectacular! Another sight to see was the continual procession of huge blocks of Portland stone drawn from the docks by big dray horses. With licences, vendors of food and drink plied their trade among the workmen, one such being John Mort of 18a George Street, Grange Town.

The firm of Gillett & Johnston, assisted by Spiridon & Co. (makers of the Coal Exchange clock) made a special report on the clock which recommended an hour bell of not less than 5cwt. Five more bells with inscriptions in Welsh and English were commissioned. As the bells were too large to fit between the openings in the tower they had to be hoisted into place during building. On a quiet night or when the wind is blowing in the right direction you can hear their chimes wafting over the roof tops.

The noble sculptured groups over the corner bays are by different sculptors and represent, from left to right beginning with the Law Courts: Welsh Science and Education (1906 by Donald McGill) Welsh Commerce and Industry (1906 by Paul Monford) and on the City Hall, Welsh Music and Poetry (1903, Paul Monford) and Welsh Unity and Patriotism (Henry Poole). My favourite sculptures are Neptune with his trident and fish-tailed tritons in a swirling sea carved by Henry Poole and F.W. Pomeroy at the base of the dome. The dome is crowned by a very nasty bronze dragon by H.C. Fehr. The richly decorated porte-cochère (*portico*) now shelters the Rolls Royces of dignitaries and bridal parties from the Welsh weather, but still receives a horse-drawn coach from time to time.

Four magnificent spaces dominate the

interior of the City Hall, firstly the entrance Hall with ceremonial staircases on each side hinting at the splendours to come in the Marble Hall on the first floor. This is lined with pairs of Siena marble pillars and white marble figures from Welsh history including Giraldus Cambrensis, Henry VII, Owain Glyndŵr and preacher William Williams, Pantycelyn. St David stands in the centre. Wonderfully Baroque doorways are framed with marble pillars and surmounted by large plaster shells and double-tailed mermaids encircled by seaweed, seductively encouraging their long hair to float and twine. One doorway leads into the Council Chamber and another into the Assembly Hall. The Council Chamber is an astonishing domed interior furnished with beautifully crafted desks and seats. The Mayor's 'throne' is set in front of a plinth supported by pillars bearing the Cardiff coat of arms and two model galleons. Large stained glass windows illuminate two sides and a huge bronze electrolier (*light fitting*) decorated with Prince of Wales feathers and little lights hung with loops of crystal beads hangs from the dome. Lastly, the Assembly Hall too is spectacular, dominated by a

The City Hall clock tower with the mermaids embracing the doors to the Council Chamber.

tunnel-vaulted ceiling divided into three bays by richly ornate plasterwork ribs and more electroliers.

Rickards and Lanchester supervised every detail of fitting and furnishing the City Hall and Law Courts using the same designs throughout. This included carved panelling and fitted bookcases, tables and chairs, everything down to the smallest item. Nothing escaped their attention: coat stands, window blinds (£180 each from Howells), mirrors, fenders, clocks, linoleum (£60 from David Morgan), lavatory paper boxes (2 shillings each) and twenty-three beds for twenty-three police cells.

The 3rd Marquess of Bute died in 1900 so the new buildings were opened in 1906 by the 4th Marquess of Bute and the Lord Mayor. The City Hall and Law Courts were a sensation among architectural students. They were a new vision and the students flocked to Cardiff to see them. Rickards himself seems to have been overwhelmed. An art historian writing in *The Observer* said '*more than once I have seen Rickards under the romantic spell woven by his own genius ... another when he took me by moonlight to see his great group of public buildings in Cardiff ...*'

Lanchester and Rickards, but

The dragon from the dome of the City Hall by H.C. Fehr.

particularly Rickards, were swept along on an immediate tide of success designing more important buildings such as the Wesleyan Central Hall, Westminster and Deptford Town Hall, London. They entered more competitions too, including London County Hall, Bombay Museum and Glamorgan County Hall but the fashion for Baroque was fading and they were unsuccessful. It was a bitter disappointment when the practice of

Dunbar, Smith & Brewer won the 1910 National Museum of Wales competition: alas, Rickards's Baroque design, complementing the City Hall and Law Courts, was already behind the latest architectural fashion which was a more robust classicism known as American Beaux-Arts. I cannot help wondering if Rickards design should have been chosen to complete his romantic vision of Cardiff's civic buildings. Rickards's life ended sadly. In 1914 he volunteered for service in France even though in doubtful health and survived the Great War but died in 1920 from tuberculosis; Lanchester outlived him by thirty-three years.

Cardiff Council has its own collection of paintings hanging in the City Hall. One popular painting is Winter by the 'Painting Laird' Joseph Farquarson, famous for his winter landscapes where a favourite theme is a red sunset casting long shadows across sheep or cattle in the snow. He preferred to paint 'plein air'. His devotion to realism was such that he constructed a painting hut on wheels equipped with a stove and a large window, even using stuffed sheep to populate his landscapes! Wits called him 'Frozen Mutton Farquarson'. Another painting, 'Hulk Offshore', by Edward F. Prichard, reminiscent of J.M.W. Turner's 'Fighting Téméraire' is thought to represent the 'Hamadryad' being towed into Cardiff where it became a hospital ship. Modern works were also acquired or commissioned, among them paintings by watercolourist Arthur Miles, a triple portrait of Diana, Princess of Wales by John Merton, and the Rt. Hon. George Thomas and H.R.H. Prince Charles by David Griffiths.

The City Hall is open on most weekdays but parts can be closed to the public because of meetings, trade shows, weddings etc. A Centenary Trail marked out with brass discs in the pavements commemorates Cardiff becoming a city in 1905.

By the late 19th century Liverpool, Manchester, Birmingham and Edinburgh had major museums and art galleries that enhanced their status and gave them a cultural prestige second only to London, Oxford and Cambridge. It was realised that a Welsh national museum would give Wales a proper historical and cultural status within Britain, but it was at least ten years before a scheme put together by Welsh MPs was presented to the Chancellor of the Exchequer, resulting in a promise of financial support and money for running costs. At the time Wales had no capital city and a 'battle of the sites' between Cardiff, Swansea, Bangor and Caernarvon followed which narrowed down to Cardiff and Swansea. Cardiff proposed a joint national museum and library on the site next to the nearly complete City Hall and the donation of the Cardiff Museum collections housed in the Old Library. This had been re-named the Welsh Museum of Natural History, Arts and Antiquities cunningly implying that it was already a national institution. In 1902 the Privy Council ordained that the national museum would be established in Cardiff, a Royal Charter obtained and additional funding was to be from an annual half penny rate and public subscription.

Edwin Seward (designer of The Exchange and the Old Library) had been working on a national museum design since 1901 and construction was due to begin in 1905 but work never really began. Perhaps the Corporation did not really like Seward's design, perhaps politics came into it, but whatever the reason it held a competition won by the London firm of Dunbar, Smith & Brewer's American Beaux-Arts design. Work began in 1910 but construction was delayed by the Great War and although building continued, a shortage of men and materials halted everything in 1917-18. It was not until 1927 that George V opened the completed entrance range and East Wing, a brilliant occasion broadcast by the BBC. The Archbishop of Wales and the Archdruid of Wales led a service with music composed by Sir Walford Davies performed by a massed choir and orchestra. The *Western Mail* called the Museum '*a building at once the pride and delight of all Welshmen and women*' and the architectural correspondent of *The Times* wrote '*there can be no question at all that this is the most completely satisfying building of the whole group ... It could never be mistaken for anything but a museum.*'

The Cardiff business community donated money and works of art to the Museum. One of these, James Pyke Thompson, had lent part of his large art collection to Cardiff Museum and Art Gallery, and after his death in 1897 more paintings, including J.M.W. Turner's exquisite Ewenny Priory were bequeathed to the National Museum together with a porcelain collection. Major Pyke Thompson had joined his father, a rich

corn merchant of Bridgewater, Somerset to become director of Spillers & Co. in Cardiff, one of the biggest flour merchants in the country (a painting of the warehouse can be seen on page 53). He engaged in many philanthropic enterprises in Cardiff and Penarth, including building the Turner House Gallery, Penarth (1887-8 Edwin Seward) which was presented to the National Museum in 1921. Another patron was sculptor Sir William Goscombe John who supported the National Museum financially and gave it his bronze 'Drummer Boy' in memory of

The National Museum of Wales, (Dunbar, Smith & Brewer) finally opened in 1927.

his wife. The Museum purchased works when it could afford them, beginning with Swansea and Nantgarw porcelain, and continuing with works by Welsh artists Thomas Jones and Richard Wilson as well as a broad spectrum of European art. The museum is also known internationally for the **Davies Collection.**

Gwendoline and Margaret Davies, the granddaughters of coal magnate David Davies Llandinam (page 40) supported

'Preswylfa', James Pyke Thompson's family home in Canton (c.1890), sadly demolished and replaced by flats and houses. In 1924 the Trustees donated the adjacent land to create Thompson's Park in Romilly Road.

many charitable causes but are remembered most for their fabulous art collection, given to the National Museum of Wales. The sisters' interest in art was kindled by their governess Jane Blaker and her artist, critic and collector brother Hugh. Miss Blaker took them to the Royal Academy and other London galleries and museums as part of their education. As soon as they left 'Highfield', their boarding school for young ladies, they began to travel in Europe, visiting galleries, going to art history courses and began to seriously collect art in 1908, assisted by Hugh Blaker. Among their earliest acquisitions were paintings by Corot and Jean François

Millet and they went on to purchase works by then unfashionable artists including Van Gogh, Cézanne and Monet. They had broad tastes and were the best kind of collectors, buying works that they liked,

James Pyke Thompson 1846–1897.

Gwendoline Davies 1882–1951.

and could afford to pay relatively high prices – paintings such as Manet's 'Effect of Snow at Petit Montrouge' cost £240. Thanks to the Davies sisters Wales has a world famous collection of Impressionists, but their collecting also included works by Augustus John and James McNeil Whistler. As well as many more paintings, drawings and prints they bought and gave the Museum Auguste Rodin's bronzes of 'The Kiss' and 'St John Preaching'.

The sisters actually lived at Gregynog near Llandinam (Montgomeryshire) where they set up an arts centre with studios, held exhibitions, concerts, and

Margaret Davies 1884–1963.

festivals. The Gregynog Press is well known for its fine books. Each sister bequeathed her own art collection to the National Museum; Gwendoline died in 1951, Margaret in 1963. They were true philanthropists.

Whilst the National Museum continues to purchase, works are still given by benefactors both as individuals and groups such as the Contemporary Art Society for Wales and The Art Fund.

From the Museum turn right into Museum Avenue to see Alexandra Gardens and Cardiff University, or left to continue along Park Place to the east side of the University and car park. It should also be possible to go into the building from there.

Attractively varied brick and stone villas continue north along **Park Place**, built originally as town houses for the affluent middle classes, but are now University departments interspersed with law chambers, accountants, banks and the like, crudely broken in the centre by the Students' Union buildings completed in 1973.

Lord Bute's engineer John MaConnochie was very busy in the Docks and wishing to improve his status, commissioned a new house from William

Burges. He became a town Councillor and eventually Lord Mayor. **Park House** has typical Burges features of pointed windows set with cast iron casements, stone ornament, decorative chimneys and little attic windows. It is given added grandeur by the arcade outside the drawing room window. The entrance loggia at the side leads into the unusual hall dominated by the back of a huge central staircase. Inside other Burges features have been kept including some fireplaces and ceilings. This is remarkable since it has been in continuous use as various offices since the early 20th century. Park House is now a dining club.

Cardiff, after relatively small beginnings, is now one of Britain's leading universities. It was founded in 1883 in Newport Road on a site previously occupied by Cardiff Infirmary. It was then called the University College

Gregynog. The Davies sisters' home near Llandinam where they set up an arts centre with workshops and studios, held concerts and supported musicians. The Gregynog Press is well known for its fine books. It is now a University of Wales Conference Centre.

of South Wales and Monmouthshire and remained thus until 1972 when it became, together with buildings on other sites, the University College, Cardiff. Then, following a merger with the University of Wales Institute of Science and Technology (UWIST) it became the University of Wales College, Cardiff. In 1988 it became the University of Wales, Cardiff and in 2004 simply Cardiff University.

A limited competition was held in 1903 for the design of **University College**. It was won by W.D. Caroe, took many years to build and indeed was never completed. Caroe & Partners was a busy, largely ecclesiastical practice: Caroe was architect to the Ecclesiastical Commissioners for

1. No. 20 Park Place or Park House (1871-5) by William Burges, who designed it for Lord Bute's engineer John McConnochie;
2. Nos. 30 and 32 Park Place.

many years. He was a pioneer of building conservation, a leading figure in the Arts and Crafts movement and a designer of metalwork, embroidery, furniture and sculpture. The University College design was intended to reflect the 17th century classical buildings of Sir Christopher Wren and his contemporaries: Caroe's individual interpretation of the classical style is described as Mannerist or Early English Renaissance. It is an interesting change from the Baroque with many individualistic features to be enjoyed, including the arcade with stone drapes enclosing the main west door and the row of Council Chamber windows framed by pillars. Caroe kept in tune with the Museum, Law Courts and City Hall by continuing their cornice lines along the western Museum Avenue elevation making the building long and low with a grand central section set between the pavilions. (*The Museum Avenue elevation is illustrated on the cover*) This contains the Council Chamber and the Library which goes at right angles through the building from the Council Chamber. The whole composition is crowned with a wooden cupola and dragon twining round a pole. From the west door one can go through the pillared entrance hall past the Goscombe John sculpture of John Viaramu Jones (1906) nobly posed in thought, into the Great Court.

It is a pleasure to go from the entrance hall up a stairway reminiscent of a Roman palace as it turns in short flights through marble arches and balustrades, round a stair-well lined with pinky-cream Penarth alabaster and lit by small glazed domes and bronze electroliers. The stairway leads to the Council Chamber, lined with wooden panelling, portraits of the chancellors and the row of tall windows. The central plaster pendant dropping down from the ceiling with its small electrolier 1 find to be a disturbing element.

John Newman, in Pevsner's *Buildings of Glamorgan* writes '*The Library, paid for by the Drapers Company of London, was the climax of the interior, a huge tunnel-vaulted room inspired by Thomas Burgh's great early 18th century library at Trinity College, Dublin.*' In 1977 Caroe's grand vision was destroyed by the insertion of a floor right across the Library about one third of the way up although this retains many original features. The upper two thirds is still an impressive interior overlooking Great Court, a space envisaged by Caroe as a quadrangle to be enclosed by a Great Hall above a gate house, a scheme that had be abandoned for lack of funds. Now Caroe's quadrangle is a car park.

There is an especially lovely view of the University from Alexandra Gardens when the spring blossom trees are out. A statue of Lord Aberdare (1898 H. Hampton)

The Welsh National War Memorial, Alexandra Gardens 1924-8 by Sir Ninian Comper. An inscription in Welsh and English is elegantly carved round the circular entablature.

Aberdare Hall 1893-5 designed by H.W. Wills of Swansea in a Jacobean style. The mullioned windows to the left belong to the panelled sitting room hung with portraits of past Wardens.

looks towards the University of which he was a patron.

The circular Welsh National War Memorial by Sir Ninian Comper (1924-8) must be one of the most beautiful anywhere, inspired, according to Sir Ninian, by the ruins of the Hadriatic cities of Tunisia and one can imagine this white temple in a desert setting, cool blue water round the base of the central memorial.

There are other memorials in Alexandra Gardens including two commemorating the Falklands Conflict when two hundred and seventy-five servicemen were killed and another to twenty-seven Cardiff men lost then another is for Welsh volunteers in the Spanish Civil War; Wales also played its part in saving destitute Basque children by bringing groups of them over and caring for them until they could return home.

North of Alexandra Gardens, the Welsh Office (1934-8, by P.K. Hanson), originally the Welsh Board of Health, is somewhat overshadowed by the huge five-storey **Executive Office of the Welsh National Assembly** (1972, Alex Gordon & Partners). It was called by the *Architects' Journal* '*a symbol of closed inaccessible government*' conveying an impression of '*bureaucracy under siege*'. What a contrast to the light, open Welsh Assembly of 2006 building in Cardiff Bay.

The plain bright red brick of the Music Department (1977 Alex Gordon & Partners) opposite forms an appropriate background for Barbara Hepworth's 'Three Obliques' 1968, and in spring, a gorgeous blossom tree.

Next, **Aberdare Hall** (1893-5 H.H. Wills), another red brick building, is the University women's hall of residence. It was one of the University's earliest buildings and its position in Cathays Park added strength to the arguments of Principal John Viaramu Jones as he persuaded Cardiff Corporation to add a site for new university buildings to those already under construction. A charming pillared veranda overlooks Queen Anne Square which is set behind a screen of paired Classical columns and red brick entrance pillars on Corbett Road.

The site of Queen Anne Square had been fields, one used by grazing horses and another as a playing field for the orphan children of **Nazareth House** in Colum Road (1874 John Prichard, extended E.M.W. Corbett 1897)and as a quiet ambulatory for the nuns who cared for the children. Nazareth House is now a residential home. The 4th Marquess of Bute, owner of the fields, wanted to build a whole private square, but only six of the neo-Georgian houses and the gatehouse were completed when the first resident, Councillor Jones, leader of the Tory party, moved in. Lord Bute apparently enjoyed Sunday afternoon strolls up and down the square, admiring the houses. He was adamant that it remain private and it was even said that initially he did not want any professional people living there because they might have too many visitors coming and going, disturbing his peace and quiet! House building was not completed until the 1960s, by which time the Government Service had bought the ground leases of fifteen plots, and the houses were occupied by military personnel.

The huge Royal Welsh College of Music and Drama was designed by BFLS Architects who won the RIBA Award of 2012 for the building. One reason for its size is the number of activities going on inside. The Richard Burton Theatre is at one end of the building and the Dora Stoutzker Concert Hall at the other end with teaching and rehearsal rooms, workshops and studios between them so that there can be a strong relationship between music, drama, and design departments. The wonderful central foyer and café are open to anyone who wants to have their coffee and Welsh cakes looking out into the trees, sometimes enjoying an informal recital. The College extends south to the Anthony Hopkins building, the former Bute Stables designed by Burges in 1868-9.

Bute Park can be entered just north of the College crossing the former feeder of the Glamorganshire Canal and paths from

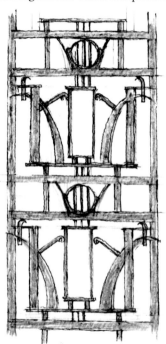

A bronze framed window in the Temple of Peace and Health (1937–1946).

this entrance reach the Secret Garden Café and Education Centre. The People's Door into the café is carved with chunky reliefs including a portrait of William Pettigrew, coracles and some small holdings that used to be in the Park. Sculptures carved into dead tree trunks can also be spotted among the trees nearby – a frog waits to target a fly on one fallen trunk, another larger trunk is made into a horseman and another into a spikey twirling dancer. Thickets of mature trees form dense, quite sinister small forests but most are grouped across the grassland in the 'Capability' Brown manner. In the spring there are golden daffodils everywhere. Another entrance to the Park is just south of the tennis courts on North Road.

Returning to the university, the **Redwood Building** (Sir Percy Thomas & Son 1960-61), reached opposite the Royal Welsh College of Music and Drama, is partner to the **Law Department**, Museum Avenue (1958-1962 Sir Percy Thomas). In a sense the buildings mark the beginning of a new era of University development: the 1905 height restriction of buildings begun by Edwin Rickards was abandoned in the 1960s when a master plan decreed a higher density of buildings and underground car-parking. The twelve storey tower is now occupied by the **Psychology Department** (1967 Percy Thomas Partnership). Part of the **School of Medicine**, the **Physiology** and **Anatomy** and **Biochemistry** blocks were all added after the 1960s.

Next to the Redwood Building is the **Temple of Peace and Health** (1937-38 finished 1946), another Sir Percy Thomas building given to Cardiff by the 1st Baron Davies in memory of the fallen of the Great War and to promote peace and health. Lord David Davies was the grandson of the industrialist David Davies Llandinam and brother of the Davies sisters (see page 113). All of them used their inherited wealth to support charitable causes. Lord Davies was an enthusiastic promoter of the League of Nations and public health, particularly the treatment of tuberculosis. Inside, the hall is lit by tall windows and lined by impressive heavy square section Portoro marble columns marked with gold veining. A striking feature is the abstract design of the bronze windows and glass doors. It is normally possible to go inside the building and see the vaulted crypt which is ornamented with floral reliefs and has a

Mid Glamorgan County Hall (1912), designed by the 29-year-old Vincent Harris who had won the competition held in 1908. The large sculptural groups by Albert Hodge represent Mining and Navigation, sources of Glamorgan's wealth.

1914-18 War Book of Remembrance. The **Bute Building** (1913-16) was designed as the Technical College by Sir Percy Thomas, winner of another competition, and is now the Welsh School of

Architecture. It also has a classical elevation, mixing Egyptian, Greek and Roman styles and ornamented by David Petersen's prancing red and black dragon.

Mid Glamorgan County Hall (1912 Vincent Harris) is a splendid building, unusual in that the front and back are quite different in design. The front elevation is one version of the classical style with its colonnade of Corinthian columns and Roman lettering, but the rear of the building resembles part of an Italian piazza. It is well worth going round to see the balcony supported by large stone brackets and with ornamental arches at each end. The Committee Rooms are wood panelled with stone chimney pieces and ornate plaster ceilings. The building is now part of Cardiff University.

The **University Registry** (1903-4) was built as the administrative headquarters of the University of Wales. Because colleges such as Aberystwyth and Bangor were far afield there was some debate as to where the Registry should be before Cardiff was selected. A limited competition was held, won by H.W. Wills & Anderson. The site was small, but the architects cleverly solved the problem of relating it to Rickards' designs: they created the illusion of a grand single storey villa, giving it a pillared entrance, putting one third of the rooms below ground level, and another third at the attic level, lit by bullseye windows. The two dragons are by Goscombe John.

Victorian enterprise and wealth pushed the building of Cardiff on and out into the surrounding countryside, often including villages and farms, churches and houses, drawing them into a new urban environment. There is at least one farmhouse up in Cyn Coed, small holdings in Grangetown and Canton, Whitchurch and Ely, historic churches and houses in Llanishen and Lisvane. **Rhiwbina Garden Village** (Raymond Unwin 1912) is not one of these, but is the best preserved Garden Village in south Wales. There are more such reminders of the small market town that Cardiff was once but I am only familiar enough with Roath, Penylan and Llandaff to include these suburbs here in my account of Cardiff, regretting the omission of much that is of interest and beauty. This account therefore proceeds from Cathays Park to Dumfries Place and Newport Road to Roath Park and Llandaff Cathedral, ending with Castell Coch.

11. Dumfries Place to St Margaret of Antioch, Roath

Newport Road, Tredegarville, Cardiff Royal Infirmary, Church of St German of Auxerre, Church of St Margaret of Antioch

The first building on the left going into Newport Road under the railway bridge is **Cardiff University's Department of Engineering and Physics**. Disregarding the unfortunate 1964 extension, go along to Col. Bruce Vaughan's wonderful central elevation of the original building, then the **Department of Physiology and Medicine** 1911-15. Decorated with twisting foliage and statues and busts of men of science and medicine, it is finished with castellated towers at each side and continues in a similar fashion to the corner where the Wyn Thomas & Partners 1987-93 extension takes it into West Grove. The building continues into **The Parade** by J.B. Fletcher in 1921-6. The fine doorway here is surmounted by strongly modelled groups of nurses and doctors.

Whilst in West Grove it is worth while taking a stroll round Tredegarville Conservation Area, although sadly, in 2019 some parts are becoming neglected.

Tredegarville was built by the Tredegar Estate over a twenty year period from 1897 onwards designed by W.G.K.E. Habershon and encompasses West Grove, The Parade, The Walk and East Grove. It feels like a city square with front gardens, mature trees and mixed uses for the houses. Some buildings are pin-pointed below.

In **West Grove**:

The former Unitarian Chapel (1886) now **The Healing Church**, oddly classical and given a decayed charm by weathered red brick and eroded Ham Hill stone.

Princes House – a description by the front railings gives full details of its history, but it is of special interest to note that it was the Mansion House until 1918 when it became the Prince of Wales Hospital for Limbless Sailors and Soldiers. Today it is owned by the Family Housing Association.

The **Mansion House** (1891 Habershon

& Fawckner) built as 'The Grove' for James Howell (of Howell's store) with double front doors and a wide central staircase so that it could to be split into two dwellings if required.

In **The Walk:**

There is a fine view of **King's Monkton School**, as one enters The Walk, formerly Our Lady's Convent School. The Nuns lived in their convent further along The Walk, now Cardiff Muslim Academy.

In **The Parade:**

The large **Cardiff and Vale College** (1897-1900 George Thomas) was built as the Intermediate School for Girls but the fine adjoining house is in need of restoration. Another large house is now Cardiff Sixth Form Academy.

No. 29, Plas Newydd House is a cheerfully striped red and yellow brick building.

Tredegarville International Church, built as a Baptist Church (1861-3 Habershon) was paid for by the shipping and coal-owning Cory family.

Tredegarville School is across Newport Road opposite Cardiff Royal Infirmary and has been such since 1860.

In Fitzalan Place south of West Grove is **Cardiff Magistrate Court House** (John

Cardiff University School of Engineering (1911-15 designed by Col. Vaughan).

Bethnell 1988-90). On the southern end is a large mosaic 'The Allegovical Figure of Justice' (Louise Shenstone Adrian Butler). A plan is available from the Court House explaining the richly coloured symbolism.

St Peter's Roman Catholic Church (1861) in St Peter Street adjacent to the conservation area was designed by Charles F. Hansom, brother of Joseph, inventor of the Hansom cab. It was built to serve Irish immigrants, refugees from the potato famine or coming over to work in the docks and construction industry who lived in Splott, Adamsdown and the Newtown areas. It was then called St Peter's in the Field and the 3rd Marquess of Bute contributed to the funds. In the early 2000s St Peter's was rescued from the pastel colours fashionable in the 1970s and 80s and decorated in its original colour scheme of stencilled patterning and bright colours to again become one of Cardiff's fine Victorian interiors. The Presbytery was added in 1872.

Turn right from St Peter Street along City Road back to Newport Road. Another longer, but very worthwhile detour is over Newport Road, past St James Church and Cardiff Royal Infirmary along Glossop Road and taking the second turning left go up Star Street to the church of St German of Auxerre, Adamsdown.

St German of Auxerre (1881-84 G.F. Bodley & Garner), one of Cardiff's most beautiful churches, was designed to

1. *St Anne's Church, Snipe Street (1886-7 J. Arthur Reeve); 2. Church of St German of Auxerre (1881-84 G.F. Bodley & Garner).*

replace an 'iron church.' It soars above the little streets, tall and narrow, supported by flying buttresses, unique in Cardiff, the roof crowned with a flèche. The interior is breath-taking. Slender pillars stretch up to pointed arches supporting a vaulted ceiling painted dark red with gold lettering

begins with Spital Barn, a building which stood just beyond the East Gate on the site of the town's medieval leper house until the Glamorgan & Monmouthshire Infirmary & Dispensary was built there in 1837. This was financed by public subscription and donations, including £1,000 from the 2nd Marquess of Bute. By 1859 the number of its beds had risen from thirty-three to fifty-five, increasing so much that in 1874 it was decided to build a new hospital. The 3rd Marquess of Bute leased four acres of Longcross Common at a peppercorn rent of £15 per annum on an 850 year lease. Funds were raised by wealthy and not so wealthy citizens alike with donations, sales of work, fairs, competitions and so on.

James, Seward & Thomas (designers of the Old Library and the Coal Exchange) won the architectural competition and work began. One stipulation to the architect – Edwin Seward took the commission – was that there should be room for expansion on the site as money became available. The interest of Cardiff Royal Infirmary lies in the differing elevations as they move from the 1883 grand entrance with ornamental gates in Glossop Road past the 1921 chapel and

and bands of black and gold. Light streams in from the great east window illuminating the nave and choir with its light green and gold ceiling, the reredos (*screen behind the altar*) and magnificent Hills organ.

The church is normally open on Saturday mornings from 10.00 to 12.00 noon after Mass 10.00am. Return to Newport Road to visit Roath, passing Cardiff Royal Infirmary.

The story of **Cardiff Royal Infirmary**

into Newport Road. Here the half-timbered domestic type buildings continue the neo-Tudor style and ornamentation which are also used in the Out Patients in Longcross Street. Glossop Terrace Maternity Hospital opposite was replaced by a huge block of student accommodation in 2019. The lovely **King Edward VII 1914-18 War Memorial** wing was designed by Col. Bruce Vaughan who also designed the adjacent ward intended for children, hence the relief sculptures of childish heads. Col. Vaughan lived locally and was heavily involved in the running of the Infirmary as chairman of the House Committee and so it followed that he collaborated with Edwin Seward in the design of another new wing in 1909, named after him. This too is decorated with reliefs including one of the Good Samaritan. His fondness for sculpture adds interest and beauty to all Col. Vaughan's Cardiff buildings including **St James Church** (1892-3) in Newport Road, considered to be his masterpiece.

Another detour is worth making by branching north off Newport Road into leafy roads of mid 19th century classical style villas built by merchants and business men as they moved out of Bute

1. Cardiff Royal Infirmary (1883 onwards), this part by Edwin Seward; 2. Cardiff Royal Infirmary War Memorial Wing.

town into greener suburbs. They are now conservation areas. **Wordsworth Avenue**, north off Newport Road, ends at **St Anne's Church, Snipe Street** (1886-7 J. Arthur Reeve a former assistant of Burges), with its spectacular flèche. The Church was closed in 2016 but panels from its finely

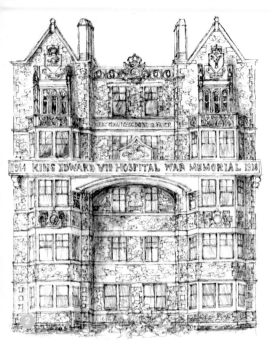

carved oak pulpit are now in St Edward's, Westville Road.

St Peter's School along Newport Road occupies the former Cardiff Grammar School, closed when grammar schools were replaced by comprehensives. Opposite are three more Victorian buildings:

Roath Branch Library (1901 Teather & Wilson) closed, is beside the site of four elm trees that are shown on a map of 1789 where Newport Road now forks into Four Elms Road and Broadway. In the 1860's Broadway was called Green Lane!

Trinity Methodist Church (1896-7 Ingall & Sons of Birmingham). The schoolrooms were refurbished as the base of the 'No Fit State Circus' company in 2014.

Clifton Street Calvinistic Church (1868 and 1880 Habershon & Fawckner) is artists' studios and meeting rooms.

The group of spires looking back along Newport Road are a dramatic sight at the junction of Newport Road and Clifton Street, one of the busy shopping centres of Roath and Adamsdown, adjoining Splott which spreads south to the Docks and East Moors. The curious name 'Splott' (rather patronisingly pronounced 'Splo' in French style by some) is thought to have come from the English 'splat' meaning a piece or patch of ground, or from 'spital' – 'hospital'. Side streets are picturesquely named after metals and precious stones and in one, Ruby Street, a former chapel has been transformed into the **Rubicon Community Dance Centre**. In mirrored studios people of all ages, but mostly young, learn ballet, hip hop, jazz, contemporary, Indian and Baroque dance.

About half a mile further along Newport Road, **Roath Court Funeral Home** (early 19th century) is on the site of the manor of Roath Dogfield, itself on the site of an earlier building. The name 'Roath' is thought to have come from the Welsh 'rhathu' meaning to scrape or smooth or, as others think, from the Irish 'rath' meaning a circular mound surrounded by a ditch. The Roath Manor Dogfield farm is known to have supplied food to Cardiff castle during Robert Fitzhammon's lordship and that of the Herberts (p. 22 & 23) and remained farm land until built on in the 19th and 20th centuries. Nearby was the small 11th century church of **St Margaret of Antioch**. The manor survived through the Middle Ages to the Elizabethan period when it was recorded as ruinous. It was sold to John Wood, a banker, in 1811-12, who probably built the present house. In *c.*1824 it was acquired by Anne, mother of Charles Crofts Williams, remaining in the Crofts family until 1953 when it was bought by Morlais Williams who made it the funeral home. One of Roath Court's claims to local fame is the Adam porch brought from Bowood House in Gloucestershire.

An early photograph shows **St Margaret of Antioch** as a simple lime-washed building surrounded by gravestones. The 1st Marquess of Bute added a family mausoleum to the north east corner but in 1867 the Trustees of the 3rd Marquess of Bute decided to build a new church and the old building was demolished, leaving the mausoleum. Using the plan of the old church, Alexander Roos the Bute Estate architect laid the foundations, but when he came of age the following year the 3rd Marquess commissioned John Prichard to complete the new St Margaret's (1869-70). Prichard's simple building in his favourite Pointed style reveals a stunning polychromatic interior of patterned brickwork, pillars and arches banded in grey and green stone and pinkish Penarth alabaster. Brass altar rails, the mausoleum and the gold figures of Sir Ninian Comper's reredos gleam in the shadows. Prichard put in clear leaded windows but they have largely been replaced with memorial stained glass, beautiful in itself but darkening the interior. The large east

St Margaret of Antioch originated in the 11th century but the present building by John Prichard dates from 1869-70.

window was blown out by bombing in the 1939-45 war and was replaced with the present window in 1952 by James Powell & Sons (Whitefriars) Ltd. The predominantly clear and yellow glass lightens the interior.

The seven huge sarcophagi enclosed in the wrought iron screen in the north-east corner is the Bute family's mausoleum, re-built by Prichard in 1881-6. This can be seen properly when the church is open to visitors, normally on spring to autumn Wednesday mornings from 10.00 – 12.00 mid-day following the 9.30 am Eucharist.

1. Roath Church House (1919); 2. The polychromatic interior of St Margaret's.

12. East Cardiff Conservation Area

St Margaret's to Roath Park, Cathays Library

St Margaret's is on the southern boundary of the East Cardiff Conservation Area which extends to the northern end of Roath Park, taking in the roads immediately around the Park and lake.

Waterloo, Roath Mill and Roath Brook Gardens form a leafy route to the recreation ground and Roath Park. In 2017-19 they were the subject of flood prevention measures which entailed the felling of mature trees and reconstruction of the stream, losing areas of the original paths and grass. There was strong opposition to the tree felling and alternative schemes were put forward but work continued. The scheme at Waterloo Gardens, the 'Sandies' and part of Roath Mill Gardens was completed in 2018 with new trees, paths and planting; a little bronze of Roath Mill itself, researched and designed by local school children, stands on a patio beside the stream. The future of Roath Brook Gardens was still uncertain in 2019.

Fortunate indeed are those who live in the terraces of late 19th and early 20th century houses overlooking these parks, created as arboretums and flower gardens. One rare tree is a female gingko which drops revolting-smelling fruits in autumn, and other splendid trees such as the curiously named wing nut tree or the liquidambar but there are mature conifers, weeping willows, beeches, and flowering cherries too. The houses, mostly of red brick with Bath stone dressings, have bays and sash windows, some with pillared porches topped with balustrades – these are in Sandringham Road. Other houses on Waterloo Road go up the hill with little iron balconies and round windows in the doors. Westville Road dates from around 1907, tall houses arranged in groups with a two-storeyed semi-detached at either end until it reaches Blenheim Road when they show an Arts and Crafts influence. The original 1915 'iron' Church of St Edward the Confessor was built as a mission church for St Margarets and was replaced by the present building in 1921, keeping the iron nave until that was replaced by the

1. & 2. Two houses in Westville Road, dating from 1907; 3. Roath Brook Gardens from 1899.

present nave in 1968. Roads of Edwardian houses continue up the hill until they reach Melrose Avenue and 1990s houses which were built on a former branch railway track. Much of Penylan and Cyncoed, developed later on in the 20th century, were two suburbs where the Jewish community tended to settle. The Synagogue in Cyncoed Gardens replaced the 1955 building in Brandreth Road, Cyncoed.

Near the group of splendid plane trees on Penylan Road is **St Andrew's United Reformed Church** (1899-1901 Habershon, Fawckner & Groves) with its elegant landmark spire. The library and community centre opened in 2009.

The Bute Estate managed the developments round the parks under the direction of their architect E.W. Corbett, but it is not entirely clear if he designed them all himself. Whoever did so showed a truly creative use of the variety of readymade interior and exterior architectural items which could be ordered from builders merchants' catalogues used by architects to put their buildings together in addition to their own designs. Every conceivable thing that might be needed to build a house could be ordered from a catalogue. There were designs for items such as carved corbels, mouldings, windows and doors, fireplaces, complete bathrooms with huge showers and lavatories. Such a bathroom can be seen at Tredegar House, Newport.

There is a fascinating variety of buildings in Ninian and Tydraw Roads, High Victorian until the Pleasure Gardens (north of the Recreation Ground) where the style changes to early Edwardian dating from 1903. Fine houses were also built in side roads, such as Shirley Road and Tydfil Place (1905). The 3rd Marquess was very particular about the standard of buildings on his land, most of which were on a 99 year lease, and stipulated that dwellings should have a bay window and gardens to set them back from the street. These houses, with little front gardens, can be seen in streets in the area between Crwys Road and Albany Road. Being of a good standard made them expensive, making for a shortage of cheap housing.

Forster's Education Act, passed in 1875, made schooling compulsory up to the age of ten, when Cardiff started building its Board Schools, but of course there were schools in the town before then. The first school recorded was in 1650, but it was not until the 18th century that the founding of further schools is recorded. It seems that Jane Herbert (of the Friary page 20) was an admirer of the charity schools movement begun by the Bluecoat School in London. In 1708 she donated £600 to

A house in Ninian Road beside Roath Park flower garden (c.1897).

provide free education for fifteen poor boys, and Alderman Craddock Wells left property in trust to fund education for the poor. These schools survived until about 1813 and, encouraged by the 2nd Marquess of Bute, the Cardiff School for Promoting the Education of the Poor was set up in 1815. There are other 19th century schools throughout Cardiff, but sadly most of them have had their wooden framed windows replaced by crude modern versions. Grade II listed **Roath Park Primary School** (1894-5 E.M.W. Corbett) in Pen-y-wain Road has its original windows, a key feature of this fine red brick Queen Anne style building.

While the roads round the Recreation Ground were being developed, **Roath Park Lake** was being excavated and the parks laid out under the supervision of William Harpur and William Pettigrew, commencing in 1889. In 1887 the 3rd Marquess of Bute had gifted one hundred and three acres of marshy land at the bottom of Penylan Hill to Cardiff for use as a public open space on condition that other land owners would also donate parcels of land. Lord Tredegar, the other major land owner at the time (he gave land for Waterloo Gardens) and others

The Infants, Roath Park Primary School (1894-6) in Pen-y-Wain Road, a splendid Queen Anne style building. Houses were built on land reaching down to the park which had actually been set aside as school playing fields.

contributed. Another condition was that the Corporation would provide the infrastructure for development of land round the park which was then dotted with farms and cottages.

Houses began to be built on embankments mostly on the west side, created by excavations from the new lake; the east side was very hilly already. Water supply to the lake comes down to Llanishen Reservoir from the Brecon Beacons, along Nant Fawr Brook, into the northern end of the lake and thence over the dam and waterfall at the southern end into a lily pond. The stream then goes through the Pleasure Gardens, to become Roath Brook. This runs beside the recreation ground, under Penylan Road, through Roath Brook, Roath Mill, and Waterloo Gardens. The brooks are often so picturesque that I am reminded of John Everett Millais' painting Ophelia. The brook then passes by Newport Road and under Southern Way to end in the Rhymney River.

William Pettigrew laid out and planted Roath Park, starting with a border in the Pleasure Gardens. By 1892 many trees had been planted and two years later the Pleasure Gardens and part of the botanic gardens were finished and the path round the lake under construction. It was opened in 1894.

Contemporary photographs of the lake and park in the early 20th century show firstly a large bare expanse of water with a path round it being walked along by Edwardians in their hats and long dresses. In later pictures trees appear, boats, bathing huts and bathers in the south east corner of the lake, a bandstand near the present children's playground and a propagation house.

An attractive feature is the bridges crossing Roath Brook ranging from cast iron, stone with balustrades and an early example of the use of concrete for a bridge. Roath Park has changed and the planting simplified, but it still has many of the characteristics of a late Victorian, early Edwardian town park. There is a café, ice-creams, boating, a playground and a glass house. It has a rose garden, mature trees, shady paths, tennis courts and a bowling green. It is recognised as one of Britain's finest historic town parks.

From Roath Park Pleasure Garden, Fairoak Road climbs up under the railway bridge to **Cathays Cemetery** (1859 T. Waring). Land occupied by Wedal Farm was sold by Lord Tredegar and William Wyndham Lewis in response to an urgent appeal for burial land made by Cardiff Corporation because of the rapidly increasing population.

The main entrance to the Cemetery in Fairoak Road is an imposing stone and cast iron gateway, leading to the Mortuary Chapels, one Episcopal, the other Non-

The Scott Memorial Lighthouse in Roath Park Lake commemorates Captain Robert Falcon Scott's ill-fated expedition to the South Pole which set out from Cardiff on June 15th, 1910. A model of his ship, the 'Terra Nova' acts as a weather vane.

Conformist, each with a porte cochère to shelter hearses until the caskets were taken into the chapels. A Reception Room is beneath the tall octagonal tower. In 2009 the listed buildings were rescued from dereliction following years of neglect but await a new use before restoration is completed.

The cemetery has a wonderful array of memorials from 1859 to the present day including those of ship owners John Cory and William Tatem. The memorials of the more important and affluent, as well as being grander, are more prominently placed beside the main paths, reflecting the structure of Victorian society. Two more people buried there met unusually tragic deaths falling from the air. Louisa Maud Evans aged only fourteen and a half fell from the basket of an air balloon during a show near Roath Park. Captain Ernest Willows fell from his balloon during a demonstration in 1926 and broke his neck. He is remembered as an early aeronaut having built and flown an airship at East Moors. In 1905 he succeeded in making short powered flights using motor bicycle engines and eventually flew to

1. *A detail of the concrete bridge in Roath Park; 2. A seaman's tombstone in Cathays Cemetery; 3. Part of the Arts and Crafts Cathays Library (1906 Spiers & Beavan).*

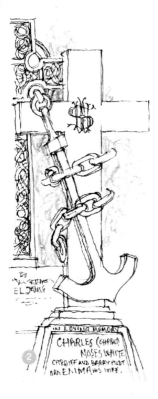

Paris, with stops on the way. Willows High School is named after him.

Cathays Cemetery has always been a place of peaceful public recreation. Leaflets giving nature and memorial trails are available from the cemetery Lodge beside the Fairoak Road entrance.

Cathays Public Library (1906 Spiers & Beavan) is a lovely example of Arts and Crafts architecture. The building 'turns the corner' perfectly with the library and reading room on either side of a central doorway. The wooden octagonal turret and needle-sharp flèche seen alongside dark conifers complete the design. Enjoy the delicate reliefs of curling foliage at the tops of the window mullions, the corner piers and the inscription over the door.

To reach Llandaff from Cathays Library take Whitchurch Road to Western Avenue, (the A48) and branch into the A4119, then turn right at the traffic lights. This route gives views of Llandaff Cathedral over playing fields. Alternatively approach it from Cardiff Castle.

13. Cardiff Castle to Llandaff

Cathedral Road, Cardiff Road

Another more leisurely route to Llandaff is from Cardiff Castle.

Until the 19th century the main bridge over the Taff was some distance upstream of **Cardiff Bridge** (or Canton Bridge) where, according to Speed's 1610 map, (page 27) the road went in a curious 'dog leg', perhaps to navigate a particularly marshy area. The bridge, made of wood, needed constant maintenance until at last in 1579 the lord of the castle instructed that it be made *'stronge to endure longe with peeres of stone and great peeces of tymber layde close over them'*. The reinforced bridge seems to have lasted at least until 1607. The bridge of today was built onto Victorian foundations in 1930-31 by City Engineer George H. Whitaker.

Sophia Gardens south of the river was given by the 3rd Marquess of Bute as public open space, named in honour of his widowed mother. The **Welsh Institute of Sport** (1969) and **SWALEC Stadium Cricket Ground** can be reached through Sophia Gardens. The first Ashes Test Match in Wales was held there in 2009.

Opposite Sophia Gardens, darkly brooding **Portcullis House** (1970-3 Sir Percy Thomas Partnership), and **Castlebridge**, another office block, is equally oppressive. Next to this, The **City Temple** (1932) and **The Westgate** (1933), also by Sir Percy Thomas Partnership, are a pleasant contrast. **Transport House & General Workers' Union Offices** (1978 Alex Gordon Partnership) marks the start of Cathedral Road. This was designated a Conservation Area in 1972 at a time when some new office buildings had already been completed at the southern end and planning consent given for a further five. Conservation area status was unfortunately too late to save some of the five threatened buildings, but not all the pre-1972 planning consents were implemented and Numbers 2, 4 and 6 survive.

Cathedral Road was laid down as a tree-lined grand avenue in the 1850s. On the southern side of the road there were plant nurseries and fields, on the north side Sophia Gardens and Pontcanna fields. It seems that numbers 6-14 (*c*.1879) were amongst the first villas to be built. At that time Conway Road and Severn Road were partly built and King's Road was just a line on the map. The interest and variety of Cathedral Road houses is endless: here are mingled a splendid progression of tall late Victorian terraces with large windows and bays, recessed doorways, stained glass, and lots of detailing, all set back from the road behind little front gardens. One can visualise genteel Victorians out strolling along the tree-lined avenue or in carriages or trams. No. 11 was for a while the childhood home of composer Ivor Novello. E.M.W. Corbett, the Bute Estate architect, designed these houses and those in streets off Cathedral Road, also part of the conservation area, including Plasturton Gardens and Plasturton Avenue, and Kyveilog and Dyfrig Streets which are especially attractive. They are still mainly private

Two River Taff bridges. Top: The Old Bridge, Pontypridd, 1756 – at 43m wide it was the widest in single span bridge in Europe. It was designed by William Edwards, twice, as his first version collapsed in 1748. Bottom: Cardiff or Canton Bridge, 1931 – the bridge is of reinforced concrete on stone pillars topped with cenotaph style obelisks and bronze torches. Listed Grade II in 2002 as a fine example of a pre-war bridge.

dwellings whereas many of the Cathedral Road houses are now apartments, consulting rooms or hotels. There were two former places of worship in Cathedral Road: the **United Synagogue** at the southern end, designed by Delissa Joseph of London (1896-7) now offices; and **The Wallich Centre**, formerly a Presbyterian Church in Wales (1903 Edgar G.C. Downs). The listed church has been cleverly adapted for its new use as a centre for care of the homeless by constructing a free-standing 'pod' in the nave to create extra rooms and a mezzanine level used as open plan offices.

Pontcanna and Canton east of Cathedral Road have much of interest too with varied Victorian and Edwardian buildings, good pubs, a free library, churches and Chapter Arts Centre. Cathedral Road gives way to Penhill Road and **Llandaff Fields** where a footpath leads to Llandaff Cathedral, with a crossing over Western Avenue. Grand and varied houses are by no means confined to Cathedral Road, but continue up Penhill into Pencisely Road.

Howell's School (1858-9 Herbert Williams) in Cardiff Road, was built with money coming originally from a 1537

1. *The interior of the former United Synagogue (1896-7 Delissa Joseph); 2. Two unique late 19th century or early 20th century houses and details of buildings in Cathedral Road.*

bequest by the Drapers' Company in London to provide dowries for poor girls. It was not spent and the Drapers secured an Act enabling them to use the bequest to build two schools for orphan girls, one in Denbigh, North Wales and one in Cardiff. The Cardiff Howells began as a boarding school, but is now only for day pupils.

14. Llandaff

Cardiff is encircled by a ring of hills. Until its dramatic growth during the 19th and early 20th centuries it was surrounded by countryside, marshes, heaths, farms and villages. One such village was **Llandaff**.

Very few of Llandaff's pre-19th century buildings survive but there is Llandaff Court (1744-6) in Cardiff Road, built for Admiral Thomas Mathew. It became the **Cathedral School** in 1958 and many buildings surround it now. The pretty chapel beside it (1858-9 Ewan Christian) is all coloured stone, with patterned slates and a little apse. **The Lodge**, No. 63 Cardiff Road, is by Prichard (1870), and so typical of his fondness for the Pointed style. On the corner with Western Avenue, opposite the Cathedral School, an unpretentious building is the office of W. Clarke, the family of stone masons and sculptors, indispensable to the historic restoration and ongoing maintenance of Llandaff Cathedral. The 'cottages ornés', Nos.64-72, thought to be by Halliday, are late 19th century. **Nos. 57-59** are a pair of picturesquely decaying polychromatic houses with basements, porches and little cast iron balconies. Chapel Lane winds up to the centre of Llandaff High Street.

John Prichard was the architect responsible for the 19th century restoration of Llandaff Cathedral and some of his fine buildings grace this part of Cardiff Road. Offices built for his architectural practice and part of his house stands beside the entrance to St Michael's Theological College. Unfinished at the time of his death in 1886, it was apparently called 'Prichard's Folly' by the locals. On a sunny day the polychromatic buildings sparkle with coloured stones, slate roofs, ornamental chimneys and the turret above his house.

St Michael's Theological College (1905-7 F.R. Kempson) incorporated the south and east walls of Prichard's unfinished house, whose walls and arrangements of roofs and gables overlook the lawn. Kempson added the ranges on each side. The dark stone **Chapel** broods

The old Cathedral School as it looked in the 1950s, before the school moved to Llandaff Court in Cardiff Road.

Mary Traynor

over the eastern end of the lawn. Over the small doorway is Frank Roper's figure of St Michael. The Chapel was designed by George Pace (1957-9), who was also working on the post 1939-45 War restoration of Llandaff Cathedral. The smooth white interior is lit by deeply recessed, randomly placed rectangular windows illuminating the vault and a beautiful Christ in Majesty made of various coloured metals, glass and enamels so that it glitters softly. It was designed by Harry Stammers and made in his City of York workshops.

Back in Cardiff Road, the former **Old Probate Registry** (1860-3 John Prichard) is in a very sober design, different to his office and house, as befits its *raison d'être*, and is greatly admired. Rows of windows, those of the upper floor in pointed style, punctuate solid walls built in just a few varieties of stone. Ornament is restrained, only used round the door, windows and along the roof line. Chimney stacks adorn the roofs, and the central stack with its little buttress and quatrefoil openings is a lovely decorative feature of the elevation. The house next door, also by Prichard, was probably meant for use by the Registrar.

The **Maltings** and the **Black Lion** pubs mark the beginning of Llandaff High Street, an attractive variety of shops and cafés and another pub. Halfway along, a blue plaque marks the sweet shop where writer Roald Dahl spent his pocket money as a pupil at the Cathedral School. **St Andrew** and **St Cross** are two minor canonries designed by Ewan Christian (1859-61). The solid gatehouse of the **Bishop's Castle** and walls around the courtyard, dating from around the late 13th century, suggest that it was more a castle than a bishop's residence. It was sacked by Owain Glyndŵr in 1404 (page 16) and just two large windows on the east side are all that remains of any living accommodation. A polychromatic restaurant in the Prichard idiom turns the corner.

The Bishop's Castle looks onto **The Green**, the heart of Llandaff village. Since at least the Middle Ages an important road from north of the river Taff forded the river near the Cathedral, climbed the hill to The Green, joined the High Street and went across Cardiff Road into Ely Road. An agreement was made between 12th century Bishop Urban and Robert the Consul of the castle allowing his men to use Llandaff ford in emergencies such as flooding in Cardiff. The ruins of the **Bell**

Tower at the beginning of the path down to the Cathedral date from the 13th century, constructed because the Cathedral and ford were then invisible from the village above. It was destroyed by Owain Glyndŵr in 1405. **City Cross** on The Green is 13th century, but the top or 'head' was replaced in 1897. In 1108 Archbishop Baldwin of Canterbury stopped there during his Welsh travels to gain support for the Third Crusade, inspiring some men listening to his preaching to take the Cross and set off for the Holy Land. The whole area from The Green to Cardiff Road became a market and an annual Whitsuntide fair on Sundays after services in the Cathedral; only burgesses of Llandaff could sell produce other than food and drink, underlining Llandaff's important separate status from Cardiff. Cardiff people could buy what they liked.

The buildings grouped round **The Green** are a delightful mixture of white mid-Victorian clergy houses, large stone and tile-hung or half-timbered houses and terraces including **St Mary's. No. 1** The Green (*c*.1863) perhaps by Prichard was built for Thomas Williams, contractor for the Cathedral restoration. Opposite, White House and White Cottage are 18th century clergy houses. Sir William Goscombe John made the bronze of **Archdeacon James Rice Buckley** (1927) who was Vicar of Llandaff for forty-five years, and Archdeacon for eleven. Prichard's dark Radyr stone **Lych Gate** marks the path leading down to the Cathedral. A terrace of half-timbered houses by Wyn Thomas & Partners (1979) replaced the old Cathedral School buildings when the school moved to Llandaff Court. Ewan Christian designed **Pendinas** (1861-63) as the **Canonry**, and **Cathedral Court** (1861-3) as the **Deanery** to the north of the War Memorial; they are heavy buildings, quite different from the chapel he had designed for the Cathedral School only a few years before. Interesting side streets of varied houses lead off The Green towards Cardiff Road. The **War Memorial** (1924) is distinguished by Goscombe John's bronze figures of a grieving woman representing Llandaff, a boy cadet and a workman carrying his rifle. Descent to the Cathedral by the **Dean's Steps** from the War Memorial gives glimpses of the beautiful west front through the trees.

15. Llandaff Cathedral

Llandaff Cathedral's position in the valley below the village dates from pre-Norman or even Roman times. Evidence for the existence of an early monastic community and church beside the River Taff comes from fragmentary remains and a mention in the 12th century *Book of Llandaff* of a tiny building with an apse at one end. A Celtic cross, thought to relate to the Irbic Cross at Llandough (page 10) found at Llandaff in 1870, can be seen in the south aisle of the Cathedral. Bishop Urban began to rebuild the church as Llandaff Cathedral in 1120. This was when the splendid Norman sanctuary arch and the doorways in the north and south walls were built and decorated with deeply carved chevron, floral and medallion patterns. The Cathedral was dedicated to SS. Peter and Paul, and Welsh saints SS Teilo, Dyfrig and Euddogwy. There are three sets of remains in Wales supposed to belong to St Teilo, one of which is buried at Llandaff. St Dyfrig's body was removed to Llandaff from his grave on Bardsey Island, Llŷn Peninsula in North Wales where he had retired to live as a hermit until he died. Euddogwy is a lesser–known figure.

The inspirational west front of the Cathedral was part of the work carried out during the bishopric of Henry of Abergavenny 1193-1218. The best approach is by the **Dean's Steps**, where the whole elevation is gradually revealed. The spire and Jasper Tower enclose the elevation with its glorious lancet windows and blind lancets (*window shapes filled with masonry instead of glass*). The West Door leads down directly into the nave where one is immediately confronted by Jacob Epstein's aluminium sculpture 'Majestas' (1957) supported on concrete parabolic arches and a cylindrical case containing positive organ pipes. Majestas is not the most recent addition to Llandaff Cathedral, but the sculpture could be said to symbolise a late phase of its chequered history from tiny chapel, through times of rebuilding, enlargement and centuries of neglect followed by 18th, 19th and 20th century restorations.

Llandaff Cathedral from the Bell Tower.

Mary Raynor 2014

153

Building work continued from the 13th century through the later medieval period when the outside walls, nave and choir were altered. The Jasper Tower (1484-95) is said to have been financed by Jasper Tudor, Henry VII's uncle, and so named after him, seemingly built by William Hart of Bristol because it is remarkably similar to the tower of St John the Baptist (page 18).The cathedral fell into decay during the two centuries following the damage wrought by the Reformation, compounded by lack of income. In 1734 a decision to bring the cathedral back to life was made by an agreement with John Wood of Bath who would construct a *'neat new conventical'*[9] within the shell of the ruin incorporating what remained of the choir and four south bays of the nave. John Wood, chiefly known for the design of classical Bath, wanted to continue to evoke the glory of ancient Rome at Llandaff, but fortunately his grand portico was never built and so the west front and Jasper Tower survived. Another century is omitted in this account, bypassing many other features that also survived – ancient tombs, sculpture, the historic graveyard and other relics – moving to the 19th and 20th century restorations.

The West Front of Llandaff Cathedral, (1193-1218) as seen from the Dean's Steps.

By the 1840s the diocese of Llandaff, whilst not wealthy in itself, was benefitting from donations and fundraising by the clergy and 'nouveaux riches' of the rapidly expanding industries of South Wales. The great 19th century restoration of Llandaff Cathedral was begun by T.H. Wyatt in 1841. It was continued by his assistant on the ground, John Prichard, son of the Vicar Choral of Llandaff. Prichard had trained in London under Augustus Welby Pugin's chief assistant T.L. Walker and was a great admirer of Pugin, a leading exponent of the fashionable Gothic style. He was also inspired by his studies of French Gothic architecture in northern France and saw himself as a 'conservative restorer', favouring the Early English or Pointed style. He was supported by Dean W.D. Conybeare, an eminent geologist most anxious to restore the building.

John Prichard's first project was to continue Wyatt's restoration of the Lady Chapel and he next began work on the Chancel by removing the plaster from the arch, applied by John Wood when building

Details of Norman decoration in Llandaff Cathedral which can be seen round the Chancel arch and the south and north doors.

his temple. As the stripping proceeded, Norman mouldings gradually appeared. An account of this event records that when Prichard was interrupted at breakfast with the news, he was so excited he spent the rest of the day helping to chip away plaster. When the Dean saw the mouldings appearing he was equally excited and said '*John, I've always liked you, but now I love you!*'[10]

Fragments of two Norman windows were also revealed and incorporated into the south wall. The restoration proceeded amidst a constant need for funds but by 1851 there was enough money to continue work in the Presbytery and Choir which were given a new clerestory (*the uppermost part of a nave pierced by windows*).

In 1852 Prichard and John Pollard Seddon went into partnership. Seddon was a London architect down in South Wales building Southerndown Marine Hotel, Bridgend and met Prichard during a visit to Llandaff. They soon joined in partnership and over the next ten years they worked together on the Llandaff restoration. Seddon, also a talented furniture and fittings designer, had contacts in the Pre-Raphaelite Brotherhood through his artist brother Thomas, so artists like Ford Maddox Brown, Edward Burne Jones, sculptor Thomas Woolner and Dante Gabriel Rossetti were engaged to carry out work for the Cathedral. Work on the nave, clerestory and roof continued alongside designing and making furniture and fittings. In 1859 estimates were given for doors and windows. Morris & Co. made six stained glass windows: the first (1866), given by Prichard and his sisters in memory of their parents, is in the south aisle, depicting 'Christ the King' by Morris;

'St Elizabeth and the boy John' (left) and 'Zacharias' (right) are by Ford Maddox Brown. Burne Jones designed the beautiful ceramic 'Six Days of Creation' reredos in the Dyfrig Chapel, with Rosetti's wife Lizzie Siddal as the model for the maidens holding glass orbs. A painting of 'The Annunciation' nearby is by contemporary painter Clive Hicks Jenkins, the Virgin Mary robed in brilliant red. Dante Gabriel Rosetti painted 'The Seed of David' triptych, which was originally the reredos under the Norman arch and is now in the St Illtyd Chapel beside the west door. He was so slow completing the paintings that the cathedral authorities would not allow him the customary finishing time to re-touch them after they were installed. In return he complained that the paintings were not visible behind the poorly lit high altar which was then beneath the Norman arch. Other memorials, carvings, paintings and sculptures are too numerous to include in this account, but will reward those who make a detailed exploration of the Cathedral.

Llandaff Cathedral, my copy of John Wood of Bath's 18th century cathedral within the medieval shell. Thank goodness he kept the superb west front and it survived.

Prichard and Seddon went on to restore the south aisle, adding external buttresses and in 1860 Prichard began work on the magnificent south-west tower and spire using multicoloured stones. Prichard was one of the first architects to use polychromy, influenced by Ruskin's first principles of colour and volumes of the *Seven Lamps of Architecture* (1849) and the *Stones of Venice* (1851). Some people thought that the tower should match the Jasper Tower with no steeple, but Prichard insisted that the cathedral should be more visible, so the steeple was built and is a wonderful landmark and the climax of the Cathedral.

The Clarke family of Llandaff, sculptors and stonemasons, were instrumental in the restoration and re-creation of the Cathedral and made sculptures of saints, prelates, Prichard himself and other ornamentation for the Tower. Edward Clarke was the first member of the family to be involved with work on the cathedral when Prichard commissioned him, aged twenty-one, to replace the Georgian wooden window in the Lady Chapel with stone. Edward Clarke and three sons continued working at the cathedral alongside the other artists and craftsmen: William carved apostles and saints for the choir stalls alongside sculptor Milo ap Griffith, and Wyndham Clarke later carved the heads of George VI and Edward VII on the cornice along the south wall.

When Prichard and Seddon terminated their partnership (amicably) each continued his own architectural practice. Seddon designed buildings in South Wales and Monmouthshire while Prichard completed the restoration of the west front and tower. His other local work includes: Nazareth House, North Road; St Fagans Vicarage; St Margaret of Antioch, Roath; and St Catherine's at Baglan, near Port Talbot (1882).

John Prichard died in 1886 and is buried in the family tomb near the south east door.

Only about eighty years had passed after Prichard's restoration of Llandaff was completed when, in 1941, a Nazi land-mine fell outside the south aisle (the spot is marked by a memorial stone) destroying most of the nave roof and the Prichard and Seddon furnishings. The Rossetti tryptich and Morris windows had been removed at the beginning of the war for safe keeping.

From 1947-57 George Gaze Pace

worked on the restoration of the Cathedral and designed new furnishings. The Cathedral roof needed immediate replacement which Pace carried out to the same external height as Prichard's, but replaced his original open timber ceiling with the present almost flat coffered ceiling. The concrete parabolic arches and organ pipes case (1957), decorated with angels salvaged from the choir stalls, support Epstein's 'Majestas'. The organ was never fully repaired after bomb damage and many years of decline made it unreliable and expensive to repair. It was unusable after 2007 when the Cathedral was struck by lightning. Major fundraising enabled work to start on a new organ, made by Nicholson's of Malvern, and it was first played (unfinished) on Holy Saturday, 2010.

Pace's major achievement was the construction of the **David or Welch Regiment Memorial Chapel** approached through St Teilo's Door in the north wall, dedicated in 1956. It was built of stones from Elizabethan cottages demolished by bombs in the Second World War, recovered from the bed of the Taff. The light white interior bears a strong resemblance to Pace's chapel at St Michael's College (page 150) with barrel vaulting and deeply set clear glass windows. The Regiment's Battle Honours, carved in very beautiful lettering by Geoffrey Kaye of York, dominate the chapel. George Pace's furnishings can be seen here and elsewhere in the Cathedral.

Before leaving Llandaff it is worth while making a detour from Cardiff Road and turning left into Fairwater Road. Llandaff House on the corner of Fairwater Road dates from the mid 17th century and further along the road are two handsome late 19th century houses thought to be by Halliday. Although fringed with hospital buildings, it is usually possible to wander around **Rookwood Hospital** on the right of Fairwater Road and see something of the original High Victorian mansion. It was built *c.*1866 by Colonel Sir Edward Stock Hill on the grounds of Llandaff House with some parts thought to be by Prichard. Outside, notable features are the huge 'porte cochère' added in 1881 and an extension decorated with mosaic panels of flowers. In the grounds there is a ruinous and overgrown little stone summer house over a vault thought have come from Cardiff Castle and seems to have been an ice house.

16. Insole Court

Insole Court further down Fairwater Road was called Ely Court until the 1930s. It was built by J.H. Insole a *nouveau riche* shipping and coal magnate on pasture land near Llandaff village which was beginning to emerge as a desirable place to live after the restoration of Llandaff Cathedral. Designed by Messrs Habershon, the Insole family and servants were living there by 1858. The house was a plain one, but by 1874 Insole had begun to rebuild and decorate in the Burges manner, adding a large clock tower with a smoking room at the top designed by George Robinson and his young assistant Edwin Seward: the half-timbered north wing and two bays either side of an entrance porch were added. The interior was remodelled and two rooms with Burges style decoration were painted by Fred Weekes, one of Burges' artists.

By 1906 Gothic style ornamentation was seriously out of fashion and George Insole, the surviving son, transformed the house by enlarging some rooms, redecorating and panelling others. The tower was shortened by removing the smoking room and pitched roof and adding a parapet, hence its strange appearance. During Edwardian times the house had a large staff and wonderful gardens filled with rare trees, plants and shrubs, as well as kitchen gardens, orchards, a peach shelter, several hot-houses and a vinery. There are still lovely but smaller gardens.

Like many other fine houses, Insole Court declined after the First World War when George Insole was killed in action, involving the remaining family in death duties. Decline in the coal and shipping industries followed and in 1931 it was proposed to build Western Avenue, cutting the estate in half. The estate was sold to Cardiff Corporation, and in 1978 the Insoles, now just two family members, left the house. Over the years, many new uses for the house have been proposed. The A.R.P. moved there for the duration of

Insole Court (Habershon c.1870s) Fairwater Road, was built by J.H. Insole, a 'nouveau riche' shipping and coal magnate.

the Second World War and now, after many ups and downs, the future of Insole Court looks bright. With the support of local organisations and Cardiff Council, the Insole Court Trust was formed in 2011 to manage the building and grounds. The Trust continues vigorous fundraising to prove to major funders such as the Heritage Lottery Fund that Insole Court has the enthusiastic support of the local community for its projects and a viable future.

The house and gardens are open all the week 10.00-4.00. Rooms can be seen as they are restored.

17. Castell Coch

An account of Cardiff is incomplete without the story of Castell Coch, another Gothic fantasy created by the 3rd Marquess of Bute and William Burges.

The quotation below from a Cadw: Welsh Historic Monuments publication captures perfectly the bosky setting of this fairy tale castle *'The uphill approach to Castell Coch is through dense beech woods, in which the perfume of wild garlic often fills the air during early summer. The soft tones of the 'Red castle' are dappled with light on the crest of the slope'*.

The castle is some three miles from town westward along the A450 road and can be seen rising from woodland on the hillside above the village of Taff's Well.

Burges was very busy at Cardiff Castle when Lord Bute commissioned an excavation of the Castell Coch ruins from his engineer James McConnochie. He then asked Burges to submit a Report of the likely original appearance of Castell Coch based on the excavated ruins. Using a study made by archaeologist and historian T.G. Clark, published in 1850, Burges presented his Report complete with illustrations of his ideas for a reconstruction drawn in fine line and delicate colours. He proposed two options: the first for conservation as an ornamental ruin, the second a reconstruction which the Marquess, entrapped as he was in his medieval dream world, chose. The castle was to be an occasional home, a weekend retreat, so it needed a functional kitchen, heating, bathrooms and lavatories.

Burges built up the original Norman foundations of three drum towers supported by buttresses (*a brick or stone mass added to a wall to strengthen it*), linked by walls and deep ditches. Using the notes and sketches he had made on his continental travels he created the medieval dream castle we see today. It is awesome and rather frightening to contemplate the buttresses and massive walls so near the steep cliff edge. It was a real challenge to paint Castell Coch as the three dimensional building it is and I found it only possible to sketch it by clawing my way up the almost vertical hillside above and anchoring myself to a tree.

The interior of Castell Coch is a succession of entrancing rooms and other spaces round a central courtyard. One passes from the Banqueting Hall to the

Castell Coch. The name means 'red castle' because the sandstone gives it a reddish hue, and the roof tiles were originally red.

Drawing Room, alive with birds and animals, dominated by the Three Fates chimney piece. Tenderly painted animals illustrate Aesop's Fables. Another gorgeous room is Lady Bute's Bedroom where she could lie in bed looking up at the domed ceiling, its panels filled with entwining brambles and forest branches; pomegranates, monkeys and nesting birds symbolise love as does the figure of Psyche holding a heart-shaped shield bearing the arms of Lord and Lady Bute. All so beautifully carved, stencilled and painted from Burges' designs, the fruits of a wonderful imagination expressed with observation, knowledge and consummate skill.

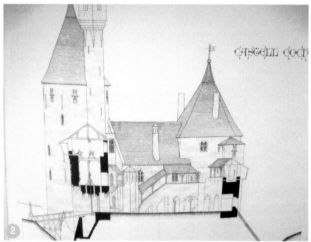

1. *Castell Coch before restoration; 2. Burges' drawing of a section across the courtyard; 3. The courtyard of Castell Coch.*

Mary Trayner

165

The designs and the model of Lady Bute's bedroom were just finished when Burges died (1881). Under the leadership of William Frame the artists and craftsmen continued as best they could to finish Castell Coch as Burges would have wished. Heartbroken, John Chapple continued with the furniture, Thomas Nicholl carved sculpture, Walter Lonsdale and Charles Campbell of Campbell, Smith & Co painted and gilded. All carried out Burges' schemes under the sad but watchful eye of Lord Bute. By 1891 Castell Coch was as complete as it could be and the Butes sometimes stayed there.

Now in the care of Cadw: Welsh Historic Monuments, Castell Coch is one of Wales' best loved historic buildings and a world-famous monument to Victorian creativity and craftsmanship.

Castell Coch is open from 9.30am – 5.00pm daily.

This brief outline of Cardiff's story by one artist and architectural sleuth ends here with regret that so much of beauty and interest is left out. But no-one is far from a historic building, the sea or the encircling hills, reminding us of our city's ancient past and remarkable history.

KEY TO MAP OF MOUNT STUART SQUARE

1. former **Ship & Pilot** pub (1881 E.M.W. Corbett)
2. **Colum Buildings** (1911)
3. **Crichton House** (c.1920) enjoy the reliefs!
4. **Nos. 6-9** (1858 probably A.Roos.) No.6. facade added 1889, W.D.Blessley) for coal-owner Sir William Perch. Nos. 6-8 are some of the original houses.
5. **Coptic House** (Ivor Jones 1910)
6. **Phoenix Buildings** replaced Siloam Welsh Particular Baptist Chapel
7. former **Lloyds Bank** (E.M.W. Corbett 1891)
8. former **St Stephen's Church** (1900-2 Col. Bruce Vaughan)
9 & 10. **Cymric and Cambrian Buildings** (1907-10 H. Budgen) replaced Buteown National School. More deeply carved reliefs
11. the giant **Empire House** or Evans & Reid Coal Co. Ltd. (1926 Ivor Jones & Percy Thomas) has a striking entrance hall and original lift.
12. **Ty Saint Line** (1900 H. Tudor Thornley) iron importers and shipbroker
13. **Nos. 58-59** (1858 Alexander Roos)
14. Flats, early 21st century replaced the grand Imperial Hotel

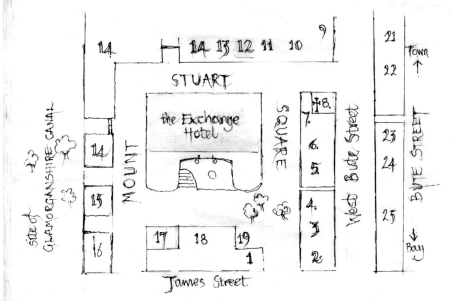

15. **Aberdare House** (1920 H. Budgen) for coal-owners R.D. Llewellyn, Merrit & Price Ltd. replaced two original houses.

16. **Mount Stuart House** (H. Tudor Thornley 1898) for shipowner John Cory

17. **Nos. 33-35** (c.1859) are re-furbished examples of Roos' final design.

18. **Baltic House** (1915 Teather & Wilson) in Edwardian baroque was the headquarters of Cardiff Bay Development Corporation

19. This 1987 building by Andrew Parker Associates replaces Gloucester Chambers, demolished in 1982 after a snow storm

20. former **Coal Exchange** (Seward & Thomas 1884-85) Listed Grade II * it was one of the most important commercial buildings in Wales. Converted to The Exchange Hotel in 2018 onwards

21. former **Bute Dock Hotel** (1839) thought to be the oldest surviving building in Butetown. In 2019 a bookshop and cafe **Octavo** and **Accent Press**

22. former **National Westminster Bank** (1926-7 R.F.C. Palmer & W.C.F.Holden)

23. **Dowlais** or **Bay Chambers** (c.1885)

24. Brick and bathstone ?19th century warehouse and offices

25. early 21st century flats named '**First Grade Care**'

26. **Cadogan House** (1900s)

27. early 21st century flats

End Notes

1. 'The Strange Genius of William Burges', National Museum of Wales exhibition catalogue 1981, J Mordaunt Crook. (*pg. 5*)

2. Welsh Folk Museum Handbook, 1962 p. 7. (*pg. 23*)

3. From 2007 exhibition marking the 1607 flood at the Cardiff Story Museum. (*pg. 26*)

4. Anon. (*pg. 29*)

5. 'A History of St John's Cardiff and the Churches of the Parish', 1997, J. C. Read, p. 35 and 36. (*pg. 38*)

6. Dictionary of Welsh National Biography (*pg. 40*)

7. Leaflet from St Mary's, Bute Street. (*pg. 69*)

8. 'The Burning Ashes of Time', Patricia Aithie, Seven. p. 91. (*pg. 88*)

9. Pevsner Buildings of Wales, Glamorgan p. 240 (*pg. 154*)

10. 'Llandaff Cathedral 2010', Editor Nick Lambert, p. 74. (*pg. 155*)

Bibliography

Pevsner The Buildings of Wales, Glamorgan John Newman, 1995, Penguin Books, University of Wales Press

Llewellyn Bren, 2006, Craig Owen Jones, Gwasg Carreg Gwalch

William Burges, Matthew Williams, 2004, Jarold Publishing

The Strange Genius of William Burges, 'Art Architect '1827–1881, Ed. J. Mordaunt *Crook*, 1981 National Museum of Wales

Castell Coch, David Mclees, 1998, CADW *Welsh Historic Monuments*

The Grand Designer Third Marquess of Bute, Rosemary Hannah, 2012, Birlin Ltd.

A Pocket Guide to Cardiff, John Davies, 2004, University of Wales Press, *Western Mail*

Discovering Cardiff's Past, Dennis Morgan, 1995, Brown & Sons, Cowbridge

A History of St John's, Cardiff and the Churches of the Parish, J. C. Read, 1995, Pauline House

Cardiff Castle and the Marquesses of Bute, Matthew Williams, Scala Publishing 2019

Cardiff's Temples of Faith, John B. Hilling & Mary Traynor, 2000, Cardiff Civic Society

Cardiff and the Valleys, John B. Hilling, 1973, Lund Humphries, London

Below the Bridge A photo-historical survey of Cardiff's docklands, 1983, Catherine Evans, Steve Dodsworth, Julie Barnett, National Museum of Wales

Butetown and Cardiff Docks, Brian Lee and Butetown History & Arts Centre, Tempus publishing Ltd.

The Tiger Bay Story, Neil Sinclair, 2003, Dragon & Tiger Enterprise

A Cardiff Notebook A Historic Records Project, 1988, City Hall, Cardiff

The Building Stones of Cardiff, John W. Perkins, 1984, University of Cardiff College Press

Llandaff Past and Present, John B. Hilling, 1978, Stewart Williams

Llandaff Cathedral, Ed. Nick Lambert, 2010, Seren

Cardiff Churches Through Time, Jean Rose, 2013, Amberley

The Tempus History of Wales, Ed. Prys Morgan, 2001, Tempus in Association with the National Library of Wales

A Companion Guide to the National Museum of Wales, Ed. Oliver Fairclough, 1993, Lund Humphries & the National Museum of Wales

Things of Beauty. What two sisters did for Wales, Ed. Oliver Fairclough, 2007, National Museum of Wales

Cardiff Civic Centre, John B. Hilling, 2016, University of Wales Press

Cardiff Royal Infirmary 1883-1983, Brian S. Aldis, 1984, University of Wales Press

Roath, Splott and Adamsdown, 1995, Jeff Childs on behalf of Roath Local History Society, Chalford

Cathays Cemetery, Cardiff on its 150th Anniversary, 2009, Friends of Cathays Cemetery

The Edwardian House, Helen Long, 1993, Manchester University

Some Historical Novels:

How Green was my Valley, Richard Llewellyn

Land of My Fathers, The Fire People, The Hosts of Rebecca, Rape of the Fair Country and others by Alexander Cordell

The Moon is Red, Myrddin ap Dafydd, 2018, Gwasg Carreg Gwalch

Acknowledgements

I could not have written this book without the support of my family and friends and I thank them all. My sister Joan Griffiths has encouraged and supported me from the early ideas and revisions of the book.

My thanks go to Professor Stephen Knight, Matthew Williams and John B. Hilling for patiently reading and advising me on the text.

I am grateful to the owners of my work for lending it for inclusion in the book and to David Thomas and the staff of Davies Colour for their painstaking reproductions of my work. My daughters Mary and Frances Traynor and granddaughters Molly and Connie Sishton have my thanks for saving me from drowning in the complexities of the computer.

The author wishes to thank Glamorgan Archives, Cardiff Council, Cardiff Castle and The Cardiff Story who have kindly allowed the inclusion of images from their collections, adding historic interest to the book.

Finally my thanks to the editors and designers of Gwasg Carreg Gwalch for their patient support and work on my book.

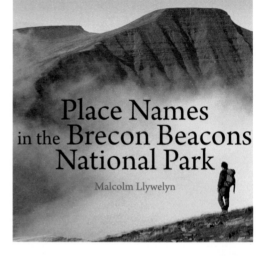
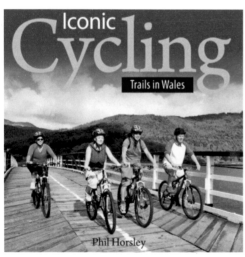
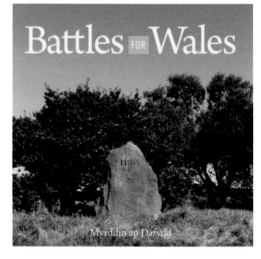